Soft Armor

The Strength of Vulnerability

by
Eileen Jimenez

DEDICATION

To You, the Reader:

You didn't stumble upon this book by accident—you're here for a reason. Maybe you've spent years carrying the weight of being "the strong one," building walls around your heart, convincing yourself that vulnerability is a risk you can't afford.

But hear me when I say this: You are not too much. You are not broken. And the armor you've built to protect yourself is not what makes you strong.

Something inside you is ready for more. More love. More connection. More of you. My hope is that these words meet you exactly where you are and guide you toward where you're meant to be.

I see you. I honor you. And I'm deeply grateful our paths have crossed.

FOREWORD

Eileen Jimenez's debut book, *Soft Armor*, opens with a heartfelt and vivid reflection on her upbringing in New York City. As someone who also grew up in a major city, Chicago, I was instantly drawn in. Though we come from different neighborhoods, I felt a deep familiarity in her story. Her words carry a raw honesty that makes you lean in and want to know more.

This book resonated with me on every level: emotional, mental, spiritual, and intellectual. Eileen's voice is both expansive and deeply intimate. She doesn't speak from a pedestal; she speaks from the middle of the journey. As a certified holistic coach, her wisdom is hard-earned and rooted in real-life experience, which gives her work a rare kind of depth.

What makes *Soft Armor* stand out is the way Eileen brings fresh perspective and deep compassion to topics we all grapple with: jealousy, compassion, self-worth, and vulnerability. Her insights feel both timely and timeless, and she shares them with the kind of heart-forward clarity that reminds you you're not alone.

This book challenges the idea that we must choose between being soft or strong. Eileen shows us that true power lies in our ability to embrace both. She offers tools that are not only practical, but soul-nourishing—gentle guidance for how to live, love, and lead with intention.

As you move through these pages, you may find yourself pausing often not because it's difficult to read, but because it lands so deeply. Eileen gives us a mirror and a map: a way to come home to ourselves, with grace.

Soft Armor isn't just a book, it's a gift. A permission slip to be fully human, fully feeling, and fully alive.

Des Stephens,
Founder, Radiant Health Institute
RadiantCoaches.com

CONTENTS

Introduction

Part I: The Armor We Build

Chapter 1: Beyond Your Safe Space Lies Growth

Life Suffocated

The Importance of Challenges

Shattering Negative Self-Talk

Flexing Your Emotional Resilience Muscle

Chapter 2: Master Self-Esteem and Purpose

Discovering Your Purpose

Cognitive Restructuring

Putting It into Practice: Visualization

The Power of Focus

Mirror Work

Chapter 3: Jealousy: The Shadow That Whispers Lies

The Three Fears

The Consequences of Jealousy

Employ Self-Awareness

Practice Gratitude

Establish Strong Boundaries

Improve Communication

Let Go of the Need for Control

Part II: Breaking Down the Walls

Chapter 4: Embrace the Pain of Transformation

The Stages of Personal Metamorphosis

The Silva Method

The Power of Surrender

Chapter 5: What We Hold Onto, Holds Us Back

Who or What Are You Blaming?

The Illusion of Control

Letting Go of the Need to Be Perfect

Letting Go of Resentment

Chapter 6: Heal Your Inner Child, Heal Your Life

Symptoms of a Wounded Inner Child

Self-Sabotaging Patterns

Low Self-Esteem

Difficulty Trusting Others

Pleasing Others

Steps to Ultimate Healing of Old Wounds

Get to Know Your Inner Child

Reparent Yourself with Kindness

Play More Often

Seek Professional Support

Meditate to Heal Your Inner Child

Chapter 7: Emotional Upgrading

Understand Your Roots

Explore Plant Medicine

Expand Your Support Network

Genetic Counseling

Practical Steps to Healing Generational Trauma

How Social Circles Affect Emotional Well-being

Emotional Intelligence (EQ)

Mastering Your Feelings

Cognitive Reappraisal

Increased Self-Awareness and Self-Regulation

Empathy

Exposure Therapy

Chapter 8: Finding Strength Beyond the Visible

Learning to Listen

Letting Go to Receive

Inviting Spirit into Daily Life

Seek the Good in Others

Chapter 9: Release Your Subconscious Power

Scientific Proof of the Power of the Subconscious Mind

Unlocking the Subconscious Through Heart-Brain Coherence

Shift Your Focus to Cultivate Greater Happiness

Seeing Is Not Believing

Achievement Without Satisfaction

Neuro-Linguistic Programming

Steps to Master Anchoring

Our Perception Shapes Our Reality

Rapport Building

Chapter 10: Fix Relationships with Imago Therapy

The Basis of Imago Therapy

The Advantages of Imago Therapy

Using Imago Therapy to Heal and Strengthen Your Bonds

Chapter 11: Growth + Giving = Fulfillment

Self-Compassion: Loving Yourself Through the Mess

Achieving Happiness Through Growth

Finding Balance for Lasting Happiness

Achieving Fulfillment Through Contribution

Shifting Focus for Greater Joy

Chapter 12: Turning to Nature

The Dark Night of the Soul

My First Rendezvous with Ayahuasca

Tepezcohuite

Is Plant Medicine the Solution for Everybody?

Part III: Soft Armor in Action

Chapter 13: Rewire for Positivity

Cognitive Reappraisal: Transforming Your Emotional Responses

Unlocking the Superpower of Your Mind

The Impact of Language

Positive Exposure Therapy: Reconditioning Emotional Responses

Novelty-Seeking

Curating Your Mental Diet

Chapter 14: Bouncing Back

The Psychological Foundations of Resilience

The Crucial Components of Resilience

The Benefits of Resilience

Practice Self-Compassion

Build a Support Network

Maintain Physical Health

Chapter 15: Radiate Charisma

The Elements of Charisma

The Benefits of Having Charisma

Methods for Cultivating Charisma

Chapter 16: Mastering the Flow State

Cultivating a Flow State

Practical Steps to Help You Enter a Flow State

Conclusion

Reclaiming Your Heart

What Comes Next?

My Final Call to You

About the Author

A tree doesn't grow where it is hard and thick, does it? It grows where it is soft, green, and vulnerable. Vulnerability is essential for growth.

–Dr. Gabor Maté

Introduction

Growing up in New York City in the '90s was a test of endurance. The city pulsed with an energy that was both exhilarating and unforgiving. The steady rumble of the subway below my feet and the blare of relentless car horns were daily reminders that life here never stops—there's a reason they call it the city that never sleeps. That same energy came with a shadow side that was impossible to escape. I saw things no kid should ever have to witness— violence, drugs, even murder. The world taught me early on that vulnerability was dangerous, so I armored myself with independence, resilience, and an unwavering belief that I could only rely on myself.

I poured myself into my work, climbing the corporate ladder with precision, becoming the woman who always had it together. I'd perfected the art of control—controlling my emotions, my environment, and how others perceived me.

As a Hispanic woman, I rarely saw anyone who looked like me in the rooms I occupied, where I found myself constantly needing to prove that I belonged. Boardrooms where I was often the only Hispanic woman in a sea of suits. Networking events where small talk felt like a strategic game, lacking real connectivity and depth. Corporate spaces where I had to work twice as hard to be seen, not just as competent, but as equal. These rooms demanded perfection, where any mistake felt amplified, and where I felt the weight of not just representing myself, but my entire identity. These rooms taught me how to navigate with caution, how to and excel—but they also taught me how isolating it is to carry that burden alone. That only made me more guarded, more careful about what I revealed. I didn't want to give anyone a reason to question whether I belonged. So, I adapted. I became who I thought I needed to be, code-switching between different versions of myself—one at home, another at work. The constant shifting left me feeling disconnected, like I was living a life that wasn't entirely mine.

I wasn't just succeeding; I was performing. And deep down, I felt like a fraud.

Who was I, really?

Beneath the polished exterior was a woman terrified of being seen. A woman who had convinced herself that she didn't need love—because love meant vulnerability, and vulnerability meant handing someone the power to hurt her. But no matter how much I tried to shut that part of myself down, it was still there, quietly waiting to be acknowledged.

Is this really what life is all about? Am I destined to always be on guard, constantly hiding behind a tough exterior?

Deep down, the emptiness grew, and a quiet voice grew stronger, echoing my entire being: "You're yearning to be seen for who you truly are. You're aching to let down your guard, to let people in. You long for someone to understand you, and to feel safe and accepted. You want to be free, to breathe without the weight of fear."

For a while, my armor did its job—keeping me safe, or at least, that's what I told myself. But eventually I had to face an undeniable truth: barriers are flawed by nature. They don't just shield you from pain; they also block out the joy, the love, and all the good things trying to find their way into your heart and soul.

That voice I heard. It belonged to my inner child. After years of putting up a facade and projecting strength, she was still there, hiding in the darkest corners of my existence. She was still vulnerable, still waiting for her needs to be met. You can bury that part of yourself under layers of emotional rubble, but it never disappears. It waits patiently until you finally turn around and pay attention.

Listening to that voice felt impossible. It meant questioning everything I'd known, questioning my entire existence—everything that had kept me safe. To acknowledge that voice meant admitting that the armor I'd spent years perfecting was actually suffocating me, which was terrifying.

So, I did what I'd always done…I buried it. I let the noise of the outside world drown it out. I kept pushing forward, reinforcing the walls that had protected me for so long. It felt easier to play the role, to keep moving, to stay busy. Vulnerability wasn't an option—it felt like a risk I couldn't afford.

But the more I ignored it, the heavier everything became. On paper, I had everything I was supposed to want—graduating high school with honors, taking advanced placement courses which allowed me to start college with 12 credits, landing a corporate job in the investment banking industry, and climbing the career ladder year after year. These were the markers of success that normally brought fulfillment. I poured everything into building the version of myself that looked perfect on the outside, but deep down, I was disconnected from it all. Each milestone felt like checking a box rather than truly living, and eventually, they stopped feeling like accomplishments and started feeling like obligations. What once gave me a sense of purpose now felt hollow. The life I'd carefully constructed started to feel more like a prison than a fortress.

And that's when it hit me—merely surviving wasn't enough. I was exhausted from carrying the weight of my own defenses. I didn't want to just get by; I wanted to breathe, to feel, to love, to live.

For that to happen, something had to change. I had to be brave enough to stop running. To turn inward. To listen.

I knew it was time to tear the wall down, brick by brick. And let me tell you—doing that was brutal but necessary. Healing never comes easy. It forces you to face the pain you've been running from, to acknowledge the fears you've buried, to let yourself feel.

And that's terrifying. Because let's be real—the world isn't always safe. People will still disappoint you. Not everyone will handle your heart with care. But the alternative? Staying walled off, disconnected, living a half-assed life? That wasn't an option anymore.

I had to find the courage to let myself be seen and embrace the vulnerability that comes with it. I had to learn that softness isn't a weakness—it's a strength.

So, I made the choice—the hardest, most important choice—to risk it. To open myself up. To let life in. And that choice changed everything.

It wasn't easy, but as I started reconnecting with those softer parts of myself, I realized something profound—the toughness I'd relied on for so long hadn't disappeared. It had evolved.

I never set out to soften. At first, I was just exhausted—emotionally drained from the relentless weight of always being the strong one. I began to question everything: why success felt hollow, why my relationships lacked real depth, and why I was constantly fighting to prove my worth.

I couldn't ignore it anymore—I needed something different, something real. So, I made a choice: to stop running, to stop numbing, and to finally lean into the discomfort of feeling—fully, without deflection. I started small. At first, it was as simple as slowing down, allowing myself to sit with my emotions instead of drowning them in work or mindless distractions. I journaled, not just to track goals, but to unravel my fears. I meditated, even when my mind fought against the stillness. I reconnected with my body through movement—dancing, working out, walking, and grounding myself with deep breaths when anxiety crept in. And when the weight of my emotions became too heavy, I let myself cry, no longer swallowing my pain out of habit. For the first time in a long time, I wasn't afraid to feel.

I also began to open up to the people I trusted, letting them see the parts of me I'd kept hidden. I practiced receiving love without questioning whether I deserved it. I embraced moments of joy without waiting for the other shoe to drop. With every small step, I realized that real strength isn't about keeping people at a distance. It's about standing in your truth, unguarded and unapologetic.

I became resilient in a new way, a way rooted not in fear but in compassion—both for myself and for others. I let go of the belief that strength meant suppressing my emotions or proving my worth through overachievement. Instead, I started redefining what it meant to be strong.

I realized that true power wasn't about shutting down or pushing through it, it was about showing up authentically, with an open heart and an unshaken sense of self. The moment I allowed myself to be present, to be real, to be *me*, everything changed.

Finally, my inner child could relax. She no longer fought for attention and could simply *be*. My transformation became a journey of rediscovering my true self; the part buried deep beneath survival tactics and layers of fear. The deeper I ventured into this uncharted territory, the more I realized I wasn't alone. So many of us put up walls and shut down emotionally just to make it through life. We all carry scars from the past, but those scars don't have to define us. They're part of our story but don't dictate who we are. Yes, they've shaped us, but they don't have to define us.

I've learned that softness isn't the enemy; it was the key to my growth. True strength lies in embracing humanity—allowing yourself to feel deeply, love fiercely, and live with an open heart, even in a world that feels so unforgiving.

This transformation became my life's purpose. It evolved into my mission: to guide others from merely surviving to truly thriving; from being hardened by life to embracing healing. Because I know what it's like to carry wounds that feel too heavy to bear. I know how hard it is to believe that healing is even possible when you've spent your whole life building armor to protect yourself. We all carry an inner child longing to be heard, yearning for healing. When we reconnect with those parts of ourselves, a profound shift happens both within us and in the world around us. Choosing softness in a world that constantly pushes you to be tough is an act of rebellion. It's the kind of courage that is beautifully contagious. And once you embrace it, you'll never want to go back.

New York City may have shaped me, but it didn't define me. I claimed that for myself when I broke free from the chains of my past and stepped into a future full of possibility. We all have that power—the power to heal, grow, and become the person we were always meant to be.

Why This Book? Why Me?

For years, I held my story close, convinced that my struggles were mine alone to carry. But the truth is, I didn't just write this book— I *lived* it. Every word is rooted in my own fight for survival, for healing, for a life that was more than just existing.

I committed myself to helping others do the same. I earned my Professional Certified Coach (PCC) credential through the International Coaching Federation (ICF). It required over 125 hours of rigorous training, more than 500 hours of client coaching experience, and a performance evaluation that tested not just my skills but my ability to create real transformation. The process pushed me to grow in ways I never expected, deepening my ability to listen, to guide, and to hold space for others in a way that I once wished someone had done for me.

I don't just coach from knowledge—I coach from lived experience. I've guided clients through battles of self-doubt, emotional walls, and deeply ingrained fears, because I've walked that very path myself. I know what it's like to question your worth, to feel stuck in survival mode, to believe that real change is out of reach. But I also know what it takes to break free.

Soft Armor isn't just another personal development book—it's a lifeline for those who are tired of surviving and ready to start living. It's for those exhausted from carrying the weight of their defenses, who want to stop running from themselves and finally step into who they were meant to be.

You don't have to go through this alone. Let this book be your coach, your guide, your companion as you take the first steps toward healing, self-trust, and the freedom to live fully. Because if I can break free, so can you.

So, are you ready to step into a new you?

Part I:
The Armor We Build

Nights in shining armour

I spend my nights

In shining armour

To intently avoid

With ardour

Any hint or sniff

Of Love

I can't allow it in

Because

If my nights are left

Wide open

My heart unguarded, will

Be broken

So, I spend my nights

In shining armour

Alone and safe

For ever after

- Birdie, 2024

Chapter 1:
Beyond Your Safe Space Lies Growth

Behind her gentle character, the strength of armor was found.
– Erin Forbes

We live in a society that glorifies a hardened exterior, holding it up as the ultimate shield against emotional wounds. Showing vulnerability is almost taboo: we risk being labeled weak, an easy target, and prey for the world to exploit. But what if true strength lies in the balance of being both strong and gentle? What if real power comes from embracing our softer side? Imagine how much richer life could be if we allowed ourselves to make that transformation.

Be your own hero…

From a young age, we're taught that we must be our own heroes, with the words "Nobody is coming to save you" etched into our hearts. Society paints vulnerability as something shameful and often mistakes kindness for weakness. And let's face it—nobody wants to be seen as weak, right?

We shut ourselves off from the world, building walls and barricades to keep anyone from getting too close. Over time, those defenses become so ingrained in our identity that they disconnect us from who we are at our core. When we're called out for being distant, shutting people out, or seeming cold and unloving, we blame society. "You have to be this way," we insist. "Otherwise, the world will swallow you whole."

What an easy excuse that is! Sure, society does present its fair share of challenges, from rising crime rates to the simmering tensions of workplace politics, where coworkers vie for the same promotion. These conflicts are often driven by a mindset of scarcity rather than abundance. In addition, competitive dynamics can surface even within friendships and even families. No wonder we feel the need to protect ourselves.

Some of us grew up in homes where putting food on the table was a top priority, but unconditional love was often overlooked—just like it had been during our parents' childhoods. We have dads who learned that boys don't cry. Our moms were raised by women so consumed with balancing family responsibilities—and sometimes a career—that emotional vulnerability was rarely given a seat at the table.

In her bestseller, *Return to Love*, Marianne Williamson explains that our parents weren't monsters. They raised us the way they were raised, with the best intentions, even if those methods sometimes missed the mark. As she explains, they felt they had to prepare us for a harsh world: "Because the world, as it is, is tough, and they wanted us to make good. We had to become as crazy as the world is, or we would never fit in here."

We've been told (rightfully so) that we can achieve anything we set our minds to. We're warriors capable of slaying our own dragons. And it's true. But that doesn't mean we must be so tough that we shut down our emotions or deny ourselves the right to feel, whether it's heartache, joy, or sadness. The freedom to express ourselves and feel worthy of unconditional love shouldn't come at the cost of our independence or personal power. Those things can coexist, and true strength lies in embracing both.

From an early age, I learned that it felt safer to build protective walls than to leave myself exposed to emotional pain. It wasn't a lesson anyone explicitly taught me; some lessons are passed down verbally from generation to generation, while others seep into us quietly, shaped by experience and unspoken moments. For me, it was a mix of both—a silent, gradual conditioning that became woven into my very being.

My tough exterior wasn't solely forged from wandering the streets of New York.

The absence of emotional love during my childhood left a lasting impression. Those early years, when emotional intelligence is still so fragile, make us vulnerable to misinterpreting even the smallest slights as something far greater. When these feelings go unacknowledged or unresolved, they become the invisible forces that shape the rest of our lives. I've come to understand that without intentional healing, we remain hurt children hidden inside grown-up bodies, carrying unspoken scars well into adulthood.

For me, it wasn't a single event that led to the growth of my armor. I grew up in a home where there was plenty of food and I was cared for, but I never felt unconditional love I often felt like an afterthought, like I was in the way, my struggles too small to matter amidst bigger concerns. And that belief followed me for as long as I can remember. I agree with best-selling author Gabby Bernstein when she says that if you believe something so deeply that it's a core belief, you manifest that belief in your life (@gabbybernstein). The more I convinced myself that I didn't matter, the more it shaped my reality—showing up in the way I carried myself, the choices I made, and the way I allowed others to treat me.

This unspoken neglect—the unmet need for love and affection—was rooted in generations of emotional deprivation. My mom, one of 14 siblings, and my dad, one of seven, grew up in homes without room for individual attention or nurturing. One-on-one time and displays of unconditional love were luxuries they never knew. How could they pass on something they'd never experienced? Without a model of genuine affection or an understanding of its importance, they simply couldn't give us what they had never received themselves.

For years, the shield I built around my heart felt like a place of safety, protecting me from pain—until it started feeling like a prison of my own making.

Life Suffocated

I grew up and, for a long time, I convinced myself I knew what it meant to be in love. I thought I understood it and believed I'd felt it deeply. Looking back, I realize now that it was never real love, because I never allowed myself to be vulnerable. Unknowingly, my fear of being hurt and my fear of being seen for who I am kept me holding people at arm's length. I'd never experienced the real, soul-connecting love I'd longed for. The kind where you feel safe, seen, and cherished, flaws and all. No matter how much I longed for it, no matter how hard I searched, it always seemed just out of reach. I felt attachment, loyalty, and an almost desperate need to make things work. But that kind of love—the raw, real, and undeniable connection—continued to elude me. Deep down, I always knew why: my protective barriers, boundaries, and walls I built to keep myself safe were slowly smothering me. What I built for protection had become my greatest obstacle, holding me back from living and loving with an open heart.

Love demands honesty and the courage to be seen for who you truly are. It calls for vulnerability. But I'd spent my entire life wrapped in armor, never allowing anyone to see beyond the walls I'd built.

Growing up, I believed that keeping people at arm's length kept me safe. I'd seen what love could do to people—the heartbreak, the disappointments, and the way it had the ability to rip you apart.

Then came the breakup that shattered me. My world fell apart, and the pain was raw and overwhelming. My desperate need for control, instead of offering relief, only deepened my suffering. I was finally confronted with the shattered illusion of what I thought was love. A connection I had felt was genuine—it seemed real, and, in many ways, it was. But deep down, I knew it wasn't the kind of love I was searching for. It lacked the depth, the substance of true love—the kind you hear about, the kind that endures through hardships and challenges.

That pure, innocent, all-encompassing love without boundaries

I didn't think it existed, so I gave up hope it would ever happen to me. I reinforced my walls, making them higher and stronger to keep myself even safer. I told myself that the *right* person would break them down one day. Like with *Sleeping Beauty*, someone would have the magic touch to break through my thorny protection, and I wouldn't have to do anything about it.

But I know now that's not how true love works.

It took me years to accept that if I wanted to experience true love, I had to dismantle the walls I had so carefully built. I had to challenge my own boundaries, step beyond the comfort of my self-imposed safety, and face the truth. No knight in shining armor could rescue me from myself. I had to let someone in, to allow them to see not just my strength, but my fears, insecurities, and imperfections. I had to take a chance, for if I didn't, I knew exactly where I'd end up—with a heart sheltered for so long that it had lost its ability to let love in.

Then I came across the words of Michel de Montaigne, and they struck me deeply: "He who fears he shall suffer, already suffers what he fears." The more I resisted opening my heart out of fear of being hurt, the more I trapped myself in the very suffering I was trying to avoid.

And that demanded bravery, the kind I wasn't convinced I had.

The turning point came during a conversation with a friend who had experienced both deep love and heartbreak. She looked at me and asked, *"Have you ever opened yourself up to someone? Let them see you—not just the version you present to the world, but all of you?"*. I had no answer, and the silence that followed spoke louder than any confession ever could. I realized that I'd been so focused on protecting myself that I'd never given anyone a chance to know me, to see me—not the perfectly curated version I showed to the world, but the real me. I wanted love without the risk but love without vulnerability is an illusion.

Letting my guard down was anything but easy. Vulnerability felt like standing on the edge of a cliff, daring myself to jump. The challenge wasn't just fear of others rejecting me—it was also about battling the stories in my head: *What if I'm not enough? What if I'm too much? What if I let my guard down and no one stays?* Vulnerability required trust, not just in others but in myself, and for a long time, I wasn't sure I could handle what might come if I took that leap of faith. Breaking down the walls I'd built and pushing back on my boundaries was a slow and steady process. I started by sharing parts of myself that had been buried for years—my fears, doubts, and dreams—with the handful of people I trusted. At first, it felt awkward, like revealing pieces of me that were meant to stay hidden. But with each small moment of honesty, I felt lighter, freer, and more alive.

The process was messy, full of starts and stops. Some days, I'd feel brave, willing to let myself be seen. On others, I'd retreat into my shell, feeling the weight of my fears creeping in. I worried that people would see me as weak or unworthy if I showed my true self. But I kept reminding myself that real strength isn't found in perfection or a polished facade—it's found in honesty, in showing up as my authentic self, flaws and all.

Vulnerability isn't a weakness; it's a testament to courage. It's the boldness to show up as yourself, even when you might be rejected. It's the key to being fully seen and understood. And yes, it's terrifying. It can feel like removing your armor in the middle of a battlefield. The truth is your inner light—your true essence— will never shine if it's hidden behind the walls you've built. Vulnerability allows your true self to step forward. It's what turns your light into a beacon—no longer dimmed by the need to hide or be someone you're not. Instead, you're allowing yourself to exist, just as you are.

My journey taught me that vulnerability fosters connection. The more I let my guard down and shared the unfiltered parts of myself, the more others felt safe to do the same...offering their own stories of insecurity and the quiet fears of unworthiness they had sheltered for far too long. Vulnerability replaces walls with bridges, creating space for genuine love to take root.

My perspective had to shift. I had to change my beliefs to transform what I'd been manifesting in my life. I stopped viewing rejection as a measure of my worth and began seeing it as an essential part of the journey. Now every time I think of rejection, I'm reminded of one of my favorite books, *The Four Agreements*, where Don Miguel Ruiz teaches us not to take anything personally. What we perceive as rejection might be redirection — protection from the universe, guiding us toward where we're meant to be. This shift wasn't easy — it's hard not to take rejection personally. But each time I showed up honestly and let myself be vulnerable, I felt stronger and more grounded in who I was.

I was learning that my worth didn't depend on anyone's approval. It was inherent to me, and no one could take it away.

I'm not saying vulnerability isn't still intimidating. There are still moments when I feel the urge to retreat, to shield myself — but then I remind myself why I chose this path: the life I'm building, the love I refuse to close myself off to, and the depth of connection I know is worth the risk.

I've realized that love isn't a destination; it's a practice. You cultivate it daily by showing up, letting yourself be seen, and embracing the beautiful messiness of being human. You don't have to be perfect to be loved. You just must be willing to be honest.

So, to anyone who feels happiness eludes them, I say, Look within. Ask yourself if you've ever let down your guard, have you've permitted yourself to be seen. Because happiness doesn't find us through walls; it finds us through the cracks where light is allowed to shine through.

The Importance of Challenges

Imagine standing at the base of a mountain. The peak seems impossibly high, and your mind is filled with doubt. But as you climb one step at a time, you find your rhythm. The initial resistance in your body fades, and a new strength emerges. By the time you reach the top, you're not just standing on the mountain but on the foundation of newfound confidence.

Training your body to do things it doesn't necessarily want to do builds confidence by demonstrating control over your physical limitations. This strategy is an effective approach to overcoming mental barriers. Physical obstacles are symbolic of life's broader struggles. They teach us the significance of discipline, fortitude, and the feeling of achievement.

Running an extra mile, lifting a heavier weight, or holding a tough position helps you build muscle and enhances your self-confidence. This idea of possibility spills over to other areas of your life, strengthening your self-confidence in your ability to face challenges head-on.

It's human nature to seek the path of least resistance.

Ironically, the easier path often leaves us feeling unfulfilled. We're wired to seek out challenges; our self-esteem pushes us to accomplish what once seemed impossible.

Completing challenging tasks expands our self-worth. The satisfaction and inner pride felt in these moments nurtures our brains into feeling a greater sense of self-worth. Self-exertion cultivates a deep, lasting sense of healthy self-esteem.

- Can you recall the last time you felt the satisfaction of completing a challenging quest?

- Was it perhaps a difficult assignment at work, learning a new skill to resolve an unusual problem, or adopting a different approach to improve your interaction with a challenging coworker?

These skills aren't bestowed upon you. They must be acquired through hard work and merit. They sometimes require a substantial amount of courage, determination, and effort. The brain operates at its best when it's completely immersed in the task at hand.

An instance of successfully finishing a difficult assignment proves your competence. This self-validation is powerful because it's based on real experiences and efforts, not external validation or fleeting successes.

Each bit of success strengthens your confidence. This internal reservoir becomes a wellspring of motivation, propelling you to tackle even bigger challenges. It's a cycle of growth and achievement that continuously enhances your self-esteem and boosts confidence in your ability to achieve the unimaginable.

Overcoming Negative Self-Perceptions

The more you repeat a thought, the more permanent those neural pathways become. These pathways shape your emotional baseline, influencing how you see the world and your sense of where you fit in it. This perception seeps into your words and actions, creating outcomes that circle back and reinforce your previous thought patterns.

Over time, your self-perception evolves into a self-fulfilling prophecy.

However, the good news is that you can alter this narrative.

Shattering Negative Self-Talk

Renovation and renewal often require demolition first.

Sometimes, what needs repair is beyond saving, and rebuilding your life on the existing foundation is no longer an option.

- When was the last time you stepped away from the hustle of life to genuinely reflect on yourself?
- When did you last take notice of your internal chatter?
- What does that internal chatter say?

Often, it's a monologue filled with doubt and self-criticism.

The more you contemplate the idea of being unworthy, the more your brain will resonate with that belief. This is due to neuroplasticity, the brain's remarkable ability to reshape itself. Each thought sends an electric pulse through your synapses, creating connections and pathways. The more you send sparks down a certain route, the more established the pathways become. That's the beauty—and the challenge—of neuroplasticity, the brain's ability to adapt and reshape itself. Just as it can build new, empowering patterns, it can just as easily reinforce negative, limiting ones.

When your mind runs on autopilot, allowing negative chatter to go unnoticed, it reinforces negative thought patterns. These patterns become ingrained, keeping you isolated from the world. Thankfully, you have the power to choose a different path. In *The Untethered Soul* by Michael Singer, he states, "You are not the voice of the mind—you are the one who hears it."

Identifying your issues and redirecting your energy and power toward solutions disrupt this self-defeating cycle. We enter this world like blank slates, gradually shaped and programmed by our interactions and experiences. The emotions you carry from the past don't define who you are; they're patterns created by your perception of those experiences. While you can't change what has happened, you can change how you perceive those moments.

Identify what is looping in the background.

The first step toward lasting change is recognizing your patterns. Gabby Bernstein refers to this process as looping. Identify the thoughts and feelings that are playing on a loop in your mind. What are your go-to reactions? According to the National Science Foundation, 95% of our thoughts are repetitive and 80% are negative. Acknowledge the negative beliefs that hold you back and understand that they're not an inherent part of who you are. These beliefs are learned behaviors that can be unlearned. By shifting your focus toward positive solutions and outcomes, you can retrain your brain to see opportunities instead of limitations.

Flexing Your Emotional Resilience Muscle

We have an emotional baseline: a default condition we often revert to.

Your emotional baseline is your default mood. Are you generally upbeat and optimistic, seeing the positive side of life? Or do you tend to view life through a glass-half-empty lens? It's important to be honest when evaluating your emotional baseline. The good news? It's not fixed. Your emotional baseline naturally shifts over time, influenced by different phases of your life, personal growth, or intentional efforts to strengthen your emotional resilience. While it may feel permanent, your perspective is always evolving—and the first step toward change is recognizing where you are right now.

I had to be honest with myself about how my emotional baseline created a negative perception regarding love, specifically unconditional love, before I could make meaningful progress.

Life happens to us all, but we can choose how to respond to what life throws our way. It's up to each of us to decide whether the freedom that comes with vulnerability is worth more than the safety of the walls we've built. And it goes beyond just a choice; it's a responsibility to make the best decisions for us. We are the ones who must define what matters most and take ownership of the path we choose to follow.

Are you ready to deconstruct the walls you erected? Are you willing to push past yourself, step beyond the familiarity of your comfort zone, and challenge yourself? Can you face your inner voice with honesty? Are you prepared to strengthen your emotional resilience and elevate your emotional baseline?

Getting Practical: Steps to Secure Lasting Change

- **It's easy to feel the urge to take huge strides in hopes of achieving rapid transformation, but big leaps are draining and difficult to maintain**. Instead, focus on consistent steps that you can be maintain over time. Small steps lead to small accomplishments, fueling confidence that propels you toward your goals.

- **Push your limits but make your goals achievable. Challenge yourself without setting yourself up for failure. Clearly define your goals, leaving no room for ambiguity**. The more precise you are about what you want to achieve and why, the less likely you'll get distracted along the way. And remember, having a plan is essential. *A goal without a plan is just a dream.*

- **Make sure you understand why you're making these changes, the benefits they bring, and how they will enhance your life**. When the journey gets tough and motivation starts to fade, reconnecting with your *why* is what will keep you moving forward.

- **Consistency fuels momentum. Expect obstacles that might slow you down and plan for them in advance**. When you anticipate challenges ahead of time, it becomes easier to navigate around them or find solutions when they arise.

- **Seek feedback from people you trust and respect**. Use their constructive input to strengthen your growth and development.

- **Prioritize rest and recharge**: Change requires energy. Schedule time to rest and avoid burnout so you can stay committed and sustain your momentum.

- **Simplify your environment**. Remove distractions or obstacles from your surroundings that make progress harder. A clear environment supports a clear mind.

- **Transformation takes time**. Don't rush the process or compare your progress to others—it's your journey.

Now you understand the value of embracing physical and mental challenges to build assurance and self-worth. When progress becomes a priority, facing difficulties becomes easier, creating a positive feedback loop that enhances your overall well-being. Remember, nurturing self-esteem and finding true fulfillment is an ongoing, personal journey that begins from within.

- Reflect upon a recent challenge you've faced.

- What was your strategy for dealing with the situation?

- What knowledge or insights did you gain from the experience?

- Record your ideas and reflect on how you might implement these insights in the future.

Recognizing and honoring the progress you've made builds confidence and keeps you moving forward. View challenges as opportunities to grow rather than setbacks. Growth isn't just about achieving your goals; it's about becoming the best version of yourself along the way. Each small improvement, no matter how small, contributes to your overall state of well-being. The journey and the personal development that occurs during the process are as important as the ultimate objective. Celebrate each victory, embrace each challenge, and utilize them as stepping stones to becoming a more confident and empowered version of yourself.

"The passion for stretching yourself and sticking to it, even (or especially) when it's not going well, is the hallmark of the growth mindset," says Carol Dweck, a psychologist and the author of The Growth Mindset.

There are older versions of you that only exist because other people give them oxygen, and you are not obliged to keep those versions alive to make other people happy. (Chapata, 2019)

You're standing at a crossroads. Maybe you never realized there was another path, or maybe you've always felt a quiet pull toward something more—but the first step always seemed just out of reach. Yet, the greatest betrayal isn't from others—it's the one we inflict on ourselves when we ignore our own growth and silence our truth.

Chapter 2:
Master Self-Esteem and Purpose

"Choosing yourself can be a struggle, especially if you've been conditioned to choose others from the time you were younger, but it's never too late to start now. It's never too late to prioritize yourself, even if tending to you seems unfamiliar and foreign at first." – Billy Chapata

What's the biggest thing holding you back from living with confidence and building healthy self-esteem? Are you afraid of what others might think? Does choosing yourself feel uncomfortable? Do you fear rejection or judgment?

That you'll turn into the subject of juicy gossip?

Be prepared: Choosing yourself might upset some people. They may not like the new, evolving version of you. Committing to your growth and bettering yourself can feel deeply uncomfortable at first, but ask yourself: Can you really afford to put off your happiness any longer?

It's Not the Chair

In August 2011, I found myself entrenched in the world of investment banking at a publicly traded holding company. Starting as an executive assistant, I worked my way up the ranks.

I genuinely believed I loved my job.

There was no morning dread, no aversion to the daily grind. I immersed myself in solving other people's problems and navigating the challenges of the corporate world.

During my time at the company, I was promoted to project manager, specializing in event planning. My role involved organizing and hosting multiple events, primarily in Los Angeles. The highlight of these events was the prestigious CEO summit, which brought together CEOs from various companies under the holding company and their direct reports to share strategies and best practices. I was able to enjoy constant travel, luxury hotels, and resorts on the company's dime.

Over time, I developed a strong working relationship with the Chief Financial Officer. As the sole EA supporting approximately a team of ten people, burnout quickly set in. I requested the hiring of another executive assistant, which led to a deep friendship.

One day at work, just as I settled into the office (I wasn't much of a morning person back then), she looked at me and said, "It's the chair!"

Confused, I asked "What about the chair?"

She explained, "You change the minute you get in that chair."

At the time, I dismissed it, attributing it to my work-focused nature. Little did I know that the chair held the key to understanding my path to self-discovery.

Then in 2019 my life turned upside down. I got laid off from a job I loved…a role that had become central to my identity. This sudden and jarring twist brought me to a pivotal crossroads in my life.

I felt betrayed, confused, and full of resentment.

What was I going to do? I'd been at this company for eight years and spent most of my late twenties and early thirties in that corporation. Now I had to start over.

I was devastated and vowed never to return to the corporate world. I quickly transitioned into a completely different industry, becoming a business development manager at a general contracting/construction management company.

I challenged myself to start over in a sector I knew absolutely nothing about. I spent three years in this role and am proud to say I managed to land two major projects despite starting out with no connections and limited knowledge. However, I faced another roadblock: sexism. I wasn't taken as seriously as my male counterparts, often being dismissed and ignored. Despite my successes, I constantly fought for recognition in that male-dominated environment.

This led to a pivotal and deeply conflicted decision to break a promise I had made to myself and return to the investment banking industry. After being laid off from a job where I had dedicated eight years of my life, a job I once believed would be my last—I was overcome with a profound sense of betrayal. The idea of going back to that world was almost unbearable, but the financial security it offered was undeniable. Wanting to maintain the lifestyle I'd grown accustomed to, I ultimately set aside my personal vow and began interviewing with investment banks once again. Within a week of interviewing, I secured a position at a private equity firm, stepping back into an executive assistant role I had long since outgrown after earning several promotions at my previous positions. It felt like a major step backward, and I quickly realized how much I resented being in that role. It wasn't the job itself that I loathed, but the way certain people made you feel insignificant because of your position. In the investment banking industry, executive assistants are often seen as *the help*, and that unspoken hierarchy was impossible to ignore.

I accepted the position to get my foot in the door and return to what I knew I was good at: helping people. However, it was solely for financial reasons this time, and the misery was palpable. Unlike my first job, I dreaded going to the office every day. The energy felt toxic. I knew I'd made a mistake. I questioned my choices daily, wondering why I was there. Attempting to secure another job a month into this new position proved futile, with every recruiter insisting I wait at least a year to be taken seriously elsewhere.

My frustration with the toxic environment, the entitlement of certain colleagues, and the overall dynamics of the workplace drove me to vent about my dissatisfaction with coworkers on a consistent basis; the daily dread and the challenge of being surrounded by people whose energy didn't align with mine made me miserable.

With every broken promise to myself, I felt myself fading— becoming someone I no longer recognized. Each compromise chipped away at my sense of identity, leaving me disconnected from the person I once was. Returning to a role I had outgrown, accepting a job I despised just to maintain my lifestyle, and tolerating a toxic environment all felt like betrayals to the person I wanted to be. Slowly, my confidence eroded, and I found myself prioritizing external expectations over my internal voice.

Instead of standing firm in my values, I let the fear of financial instability and societal pressures guide my choices. I stopped listening to my intuition and started living on autopilot, going through the motions of a life that no longer felt authentic. The spark I once had—the one that came from pursuing my passions and building a life I loved—dimmed under the weight of settling for what felt safe, even if it was overpowering me.

In that process, I began to forget what mattered to me. My dreams felt distant, my voice quieter, and my sense of purpose blurred. The more I stayed in this space, the further I drifted from the version of myself who believed in the power of choosing happiness and fulfillment over fear and comfort. It was like watching myself disappear in slow motion, and I knew something had to change. I tried everything. I began meditating daily, working out, reciting daily affirmations, and going to therapy, but nothing seemed to work. I was no longer my fun-loving outing self; I was constantly irritable and agitated.

I hated who I had become but never gave up on hope.

I knew there was a reason my soul led me on this journey, and I was determined to find it. Six months into this cycle, a glimmer of hope emerged–a mentoring program was introduced to the company. Eager for guidance, I quickly signed up. Among the mentors, an African American managing director caught my eye. Being a Hispanic woman in the investment banking industry, I often felt alone, misunderstood, and isolated in my career. I chose this person, hoping that our shared marginalized backgrounds would allow us to relate on a different level.

My instincts were right! We immediately connected. He understood my struggles and frustrations, displaying openness, honesty, and vulnerability–qualities you'd expect in a mentor.

During one of our mentoring sessions, he shared a vision: "I can see you being a life coach." Despite my initial resistance, fueled by a dislike for social media and a desire for privacy, the seed was planted.

Days passed, and I found myself unable to shake his words. Could I become a life coach? Reflecting on my love for human behavior, psychology, spirituality, and leadership, I realized I'd been coaching friends and family, executives, and partners my entire life. I'd always been the person others leaned on for advice and support.

Despite telling myself I had no clear passion or life purpose, the signs were right before me. My entire life had inadvertently prepared me for the role of a life coach.

My soul, yearning for change, guided me toward my life's purpose, urging me to leave behind everything I despised. With newfound clarity, I searched for an accredited school and began my life coaching journey.

I stumbled across *Radiant Coaches Academy,* and immediately after my first call with Dez Stephens, the founder, I knew *Radiant Academy* was where I belonged. It was exactly what my soul had been craving—an inclusive, supportive community of like-minded people, all driven by a shared calling to serve the world.

So, was it the chair?

Paradoxically, yes and no, the answer mainly depends on how I perceive my story and the nature of my inner narrative. In its symbolic form, the chair represented everything I loathed, every compromise I made, and every aspect of my soul that yearned for something more. I could've easily blamed external factors for the misery I experienced. But shifting the blame and placing the source of my struggles outside myself would mean surrendering my power—and that was something I wasn't willing to do. It might have been the path of least resistance, but ultimately, it wouldn't have led to my emotional, spiritual, and mental growth.

Ultimately, the chair wasn't just a piece of office furniture. As I looked within, it became the compass directing me toward a more fulfilling, rewarding journey where I could leverage my experiences to help others and be of service. This transition from investment banking to life coaching has been a tumultuous yet enlightening journey. As I embraced the coaching path, I carried with me the lessons learned from each chapter of my life.

Sometimes, the most profound insights come from the most unexpected places—even something as ordinary as an office chair.

The chair, once easily a symbol of discontent, now stands as a testament to the resilience of the human spirit and the unwavering pursuit of one's true calling. My narrative continues to evolve, with each word echoing the resilience and determination that fuel my journey toward a more meaningful existence.

The Compass Within: Finding Your Purpose

There comes a time in life when you find yourself asking, *Is this it?* Maybe it's while sitting in a crowded office, stuck in traffic, or lying awake at night, staring at the ceiling. It's the kind of question that sneaks up on you, tugging at the edges of the life you thought you wanted. The truth is, finding your purpose isn't about chasing some grand, predefined destiny. It's about discovering the quiet truth that's been inside you all along—the internal compass that's been guiding you, even when you didn't realize it.

Letting Go of the "One Purpose" Myth

First, let's dispel the myth: you don't have a singular purpose. I learned the purpose isn't a job title, a milestone, or a reward waiting for you at the end of some journey. It's a living, breathing force that evolves as you do. The pressure to find *the one thing* you're meant to do can leave you feeling overwhelmed and stuck. Instead, think of purpose as a thread that runs through your life, weaving together your passions, skills, and experiences in a way that feels fulfilling and true to who you are.

When I lost my job, the identity I had carefully built around my career came crashing down, forcing me to confront an uncomfortable truth: I had mistaken achievement for purpose. I was so focused on *what* I was doing that I forgot to ask myself *why* I was doing it. Purpose isn't about what you accomplish—it's about the impact you want to have and the way you want to show up in the world.

Tuning Into Your Inner Compass

Finding your purpose starts with turning inward and asking
yourself some hard, honest questions:

- What lights me up?

- What are the things that make me lose track of time?

- What breaks my heart?

- What challenges or injustices stir something deep within
  me?

- Who am I when no one is watching?

- What feels authentic when I'm not trying to prove
  anything to anyone?

The answers to these questions aren't always immediate or
obvious, but they're already within you. Purpose isn't something
you go out and find—it's something you uncover by peeling back
layers of fear, societal expectations, and self-doubt.

Following the Breadcrumbs

Purpose doesn't arrive in a flash of clarity; it reveals itself in
pieces. You'll notice it in the hobbies you love, the causes you feel
passionate about, or the compliments you hear most often. These
are the breadcrumbs. Follow them. Experiment. Try new things,
even if they don't fit neatly into a plan. Purpose often emerges not
from certainty, but from curiosity and action.

For me, it began with a simple realization: I felt most alive when I
was helping others. Whether I was offering advice or guiding
someone through a challenge, those moments of connection made
me feel aligned and whole. Over time, I realized my purpose

wasn't tied to a specific job or title—it was about inspiring, connecting, and supporting others on their journeys.

Redefining Success

Living your purpose requires redefining what success means. True success lies in alignment—living in a way that reflects your values and prioritizing the things that matter most to you.

The Power of Starting Small

Finding your purpose doesn't require a grand overhaul of your life. It begins with small, deliberate steps. Volunteer for a cause that speaks to you. Take a class that sparks your curiosity. Start journaling to connect with your thoughts and see where they lead. The key is to act, even if you don't have all the answers yet. Purpose unfolds through doing.

Embracing Purpose as a Journey

Your purpose will grow and change alongside you. What inspires you today may look entirely different a decade from now, and that's okay. Purpose is more about the journey of becoming. It's about checking in with yourself, asking if you're living in alignment with what matters most, and being willing to adjust your course when necessary.

The beauty of purpose lies in the journey. It's about leaning into the things that make you feel most alive and trusting that piece by piece, the bigger picture will come together.

Start right where you are. Listen to your inner compass, and trust that every step, even the uncertain ones, is bringing you closer to the life you're meant to live.

Discovering Your Purpose

Discovering your purpose takes time, and it reveals itself through a combination of action and self-reflection.

- Reflect on the moments in your life when you felt most fulfilled.

- Look for the common threads or activities that brought you that sense of joy and purpose.

- Write a personal mission statement. It should capture your purpose and guide your decisions and actions in the future.

Dissecting a Core Belief

When I entered the life coaching realm, I was often asked, "Who is your ideal client?"

It might seem like a simple question, but the answer carries real weight. My mentors taught me early on that understanding my ideal client is just as important as setting clear goals. Without this clarity, I'd be shooting from the hip without making a meaningful contribution to anyone's life. Defining my client avatar was essential to my practice and my quest to serve the world.

Initially, my instinctive answer was always men. I was focused on my healthy connections with the men in my life. I grew up with boys. I had several male best friends growing up. When I thought about women as my ideal clients, my perception was clouded by an unresolved mother wound that still required healing. My hesitance had little to do with my ability to connect with women and everything to do with the lens through which I viewed those relationships.

Over time, my growing need for clarity forced me to question this belief. Had I really struggled to connect with women, or had I not examined the depth of those connections? When I took a deep, honest look at all my relationships, I realized something crucial: I had many strong, fulfilling connections with women—some of whom I considered sisters. These bonds, built over decades, were rooted in acceptance, support, and trust.

I then shifted my attention outward, seeking valuable feedback from others on where they believed my strengths should be directed. I asked my friends, colleagues, and mentors how they experienced me as a coach, as a friend, and as a trusted confidante. Their responses were eye-opening. Women frequently told me that my ability to create a safe space, to listen without judgment, and to hold them through their emotional processing was invaluable. Without realizing it, I had been offering women the same qualities that had always felt effortless when working with men.

Then it hit me: the belief that I couldn't work with women was a false assumption that had gone unchallenged for too long. Once I allowed myself to step back and reassess, I saw the reality: I had just as many cherished and meaningful relationships with women as I did with men. The belief that I was more suited to work with men was an illusion, shattered by the power of asking the right questions and being open to the answers.

How You Can Do the Same

The beliefs we hold about ourselves often feel like truth, but many of them are outdated stories we've been telling ourselves for years. The good news? You can rewrite the script. Here's how:

1. **Identify the Belief** – What is a limiting belief you have about yourself? It could be related to your relationships, your career, or your self-worth. Write it down.

2. **Question Its Validity** – Ask yourself: Where did this belief come from? Is it based on actual evidence, or is it something you assumed to be true? Have you ever challenged it?

3. **Gather Contradicting Evidence** – Just like I realized I had meaningful relationships with women, you need to find real-life examples that prove your belief to be incorrect. Have there been times where you've succeeded despite your doubts? Have people given you feedback that contradicts your assumption?

4. **Seek Outside Perspectives** – Turn to close friends, mentors, or colleagues for their perspective on how they see you. Sometimes, we're too caught up in our own beliefs to recognize the truth, but those around us can provide clarity and insight we might otherwise overlook.

5. **Reframe the Narrative** – Swap the limiting belief for an empowering one. Instead of saying, "I'm not good at forming deep connections," reframe it as, "I am capable of building meaningful relationships when I show up as my authentic self."

6. **Take Small, Aligned Actions** – Start embodying your new belief through action. If you've always thought you weren't brave, do something that scares you. If you've believed you struggle with deep connections, make the first move in a meaningful conversation. Change happens when you start living as the version of yourself you want to become.

Imagine your negative self-perceptions as the tabletop of a structure. While the tabletop may seem like the most prominent part, without its legs, it's useless. The questions you ask to challenge the validity of these perceptions act as tools to cut away those legs. If the beliefs propping up your self-perception aren't true or valid, your questions will break them down, causing the tabletop—your negative belief—to collapse. When that happens, it's time to replace the negative perception with a positive one!

In many cases, the unfounded negative thoughts that occupy your mind can be swapped out for positive affirmations when you consciously shift your focus. Recognizing these destructive patterns and questioning their truth creates room for new, empowering beliefs. It takes patience and repetition, but with commitment, the negative voices running the show get drowned out by affirmations that celebrate your strengths and your potential.

So, ask yourself—what beliefs about yourself have gone unchallenged for too long? And are you ready to confront them?

Cognitive Restructuring

It begins with identifying a belief that feels limiting or harmful—this often shows up as a recurring thought or feeling during challenges or moments of doubt. Once identified, the next step is to explore the origin of the belief. Was it shaped by childhood experiences, societal pressures, or repeated failures? Understanding where it came from helps to view it as something learned, rather than an unchangeable truth.

The next phase involves challenging the belief by asking critical questions: *Is this always true? Do I have evidence that disproves this? What would I say to a friend who held this belief?* This reframing creates space to replace the limiting belief with one that is more empowering and aligned with personal growth. For example: shifting from *I'm not good enough* to *I am capable and learning every day.*

Finally, test and reinforce the new belief. This can be done through small, consistent actions that align with the new belief, such as setting achievable goals, practicing affirmations, or journaling. By acting as though the new belief is true, evidence builds over time, reinforcing the transformation. The process is iterative, requiring regular reflection and adjustment as needed, but it's a powerful tool for personal growth and self-awareness.

Live in the end.

Neville Goddard was a spiritual teacher and author who taught the power of imagination and the importance of living in the end to shape our reality.

"When a man learns the art of thinking from the end, that man is master of his fate. For he defines his end, he formulates an aim in life and then feels himself right into the situation of that end."

But what does this really mean? *Living in the en*d is the idea that to achieve your desired outcome, you need to envision it as if it already exists. By mentally immersing yourself in this reality, it influences your actions and words as though it has already come to pass.

Visualization

To clarify this concept, let's use the example of landing your dream job. Imagine you want to be a successful entrepreneur. The idea of living in the end means that you must visualize yourself as already running a thriving business. Picture yourself confidently making decisions, networking with industry leaders, and leading your team purposefully. What do you do every morning? How do you dress? What do you do before bed? *Feel yourself* as already living the life of a fruitful entrepreneur. By immersing yourself in this feeling and mental image, you'll naturally make choices that align with your vision, such as investing in your skills, seeking out mentorship, or taking calculated risks. Acting as if you've already achieved your desire sets the stage for the reality to unfold.

Visualization is powerful because the mind struggles to distinguish between vividly imagined scenarios and reality. When you immerse yourself in the details—seeing, hearing and, most importantly, feeling your desired outcome—you create a deeper emotional connection. The stronger the feeling, the more real it becomes, naturally aligning your thoughts and actions with that vision until it unfolds in your reality.

Putting It into Practice: Visualization

- Find a quiet space, close your eyes, and picture yourself successfully overcoming a challenge.

- Imagine every detail *of the end* as vividly as you can. Feel the rush of emotions that come with achieving your goal— the joy, the pride, the pure satisfaction. Take in the smells, the sights, and the sounds around you. Think about how you'll act differently, how others will treat you, and how your sense of self will transform.

- Engage in this visualization exercise regularly to strengthen your belief. Place reminders of your visualization in strategic places. A vision board can also be immensely helpful in this process.

Fully immerse yourself in each session, allowing yourself to deeply engage and enjoy the process. Pay attention to the shifts that unfold along the way. The more vivid and frequent your visualizations, the more powerful their impact—and the closer you get to your desired outcome.

The Power of Focus

Being present seems simple, yet it's one of the hardest skills to master. How often do we drift into the past, worry about the future, or move through life on autopilot? We miss the quiet, meaningful moments—the ones that hold the potential for real joy—because we're too focused on chasing grand, picture-perfect milestones, believing they'll finally complete us. But what if everything we're searching for is already here, waiting to be noticed? *It all begins with embracing the present moment.*

Isn't it wild how often we're mentally checked out—stuck in the past, anxious about the future, or just coasting through life on autopilot? We miss the small, meaningful moments that could light us up because we're too busy chasing after the big, shiny ones we believe will make everything perfect.

There are moments in life when everything feels still—whether it's sitting in quiet reflection, enjoying a simple meal, or feeling the warmth of the sun on your skin. These moments aren't extraordinary because of where they happen but because of the choice to fully experience them. That's the magic of presence. When you truly show up for your life, without distractions or the need to prove anything, you allow yourself to feel the richness of the present moment. And in that space, your light begins to shine—not from seeking validation, but simply from being fully, unapologetically yourself.

Focusing on the present moment is deeply transformative, echoing the wisdom found in Buddhist teachings. Buddhism emphasizes the importance of present-centered awareness, which helps individuals see themselves as they truly are without self-judgment.

By focusing on the present moment while finding value in our actions and thoughts, we can better recognize and appreciate our own worth.

This mindful focus helps to dismantle the internal narratives of inadequacy and unworthiness, replacing them with a deep, unwavering sense of self-acceptance and compassion.

The Buddhist art of focused attention teaches us that by directing our awareness inward with kindness and clarity, we can uncover and nurture our inherent self-worth, leading to a more confident and fulfilled life. This inner transformation naturally enhances self-esteem, empowering us to live more fully, achieve our dreams, and step bravely into spaces where vulnerability becomes effortless.

Every thought we have at any given moment falls into one of these categories:

1. Thoughts centered on what is missing or what you already have in your life.

2. Thoughts dwelling on the past, observing the present, or anticipating the future.

3. Thoughts about what lies beyond your control or what is within your power to change.

Focusing on *what you have* and *what you can control in the present moment* is a powerful way to elevate your self-esteem. It keeps you grounded and genuinely lets you appreciate your progress and growth.

Practical Guidance: Shifting Your Focus

Take a moment to center your thoughts in the present moment. Pick up any object nearby—a pen, an apple, or whatever is within reach.

Notice the texture under your fingers, the weight in your hand, and the color and details of its surface. Inhale and observe any scent it may have. Think about where it came from and how you might use it. For instance, if it's an apple, you can also use it as a paperweight or a ball. If you can taste it, go ahead and do so. For the next two or three minutes, let your full attention rest solely on the object and your current experience with it.

See how effortless it can be to stay present in the moment? Even the most disciplined minds find it challenging to maintain this focus sometimes, but with patience and consistent practice, it'll become second nature.

Let's move on to stage two of practice.

- Reflect on the qualities and attributes you appreciate most about yourself. Recall a time when you acted in alignment with these qualities. How did it make you feel? What were the outcomes? How did others respond when you stayed true to yourself?

- When your mind drifts toward negativity, acknowledge the thoughts and then intentionally redirect your focus to the positive aspects of your day. Do this as often as needed throughout the day.

- Finally, set aside time at the end of the day to reflect on your accomplishments and positive experiences. Let these uplifting thoughts settle in as you peacefully drift off to sleep.

Mirror Work

Your mind will always work to validate your beliefs about your own unworthiness. To shine brighter, you must learn to let go.

To break this cycle, pursuing self-love and self-acceptance is essential. True virtue doesn't mean perfection; it means recognizing and embracing your authentic self.

You can't shine when you're weighed down by burdens that were never yours to carry. Letting go isn't a one time act; it's a daily commitment. It means continually choosing to release whatever dims your light—whether it's the need to prove yourself, the fear of others' opinions, or the outdated stories you tell yourself about not being good enough.

Consistently acknowledging your worth daily is essential for building self-confidence and maintaining a strong sense of self.

As you gaze into the mirror, affirm your worthiness for love, success, and happiness. Louise Hay, author of *Mirror Work*, championed this transformative practice to overcome anxiety and self-doubt. Speaking affirmations like "I am worthy" or "I love and accept myself" while looking into your own eyes creates a profound shift—helping you replace self-criticism with self-compassion and build genuine confidence from within.

Hay, a pioneer in self-help, emphasized that mirror work helps dissolve negative self-talk and builds self-esteem. Scientifically, mirror work is rooted in neuroplasticity—the brain's ability to reorganize itself and form new neural pathways through repeated thought patterns.

Looking into your own eyes while affirming positive beliefs creates a deeper emotional connection and reinforces the belief. Integrating mirror work into your daily routine can significantly improve your mental health, fostering a sense of calm and confidence. Your affirmations will slowly be embedded into your subconscious mind, transforming the lens through which you perceive your external world.

Practical Application: Affirming Your Self-Worth

The only thing standing between you and your excellence is your resistance to acknowledging and accepting it. Your light has always been there, waiting for you to step aside, let go, and let it shine.

- Write a set of affirmations that strengthen your commitment to personal growth and self-improvement.

- Then, make mirror work part of your daily routine: stand in front of the mirror, look yourself straight in the eyes, and speak affirmations with conviction and confidence.

Here are some to inspire you:

"I am deserving of all the great things life has to offer."

"I am deserving of love and respect."

"I am worthy of all the good life has to offer."

Which affirmations resonate with you the most?

Step into the freedom to be unapologetically you.

When you finally let yourself glow from the inside out, it's not just about changing how the world sees you but transforming how you see yourself. That glow brings a sense of peace that holds steady even when everything around you feels chaotic and a strength that comes from knowing you're enough, exactly as you are. It's about being whole and letting the real you shine through.

Stop shrinking yourself to fit into someone else's mold.

Don't hold back. Let yourself shine in all your messy, beautiful glory. Your glow isn't something you must earn or search for— it's already within you, waiting for you to let it radiate.

Chapter 3:
Jealousy: The Shadow That Whispers Lies

"Jealousy is a cover-up emotion. It presents as anger or judgment, when in reality it is sadness and self-satisfaction."
— Brianna Wiest

Why does jealousy feel easier to name when we dress it up in metaphor? Is it because disguising it in poetic language makes it seem less raw, less uncomfortable to face? Jealousy is a powerful emotion that has been depicted across various forms of media, resonating with many due to its universal nature. In Disney's *Snow White and the Seven Dwarfs*, the Evil Queen's envy of Snow White's beauty drives her to malicious actions, highlighting how jealousy can lead to destructive behavior. Likewise, in *The Great Gatsby*, Tom Buchanan's jealousy over Daisy's affection for Gatsby fuels his resentment, ultimately leading to devastating consequences. These portrayals underscore how jealousy can cloud judgment and strain relationships, prompting us to reflect on its impact in our own lives.

But why does jealousy have such a powerful grip on us, distorting our thoughts and emotions? How does it creep in so quietly, only to take complete control?

Jealousy has such a powerful grip on us because it taps into our deepest fears—fear of not being enough, fear of loss, and fear of being replaced. It distorts our thoughts by magnifying insecurities and convincing us that what we have isn't enough or that someone else has something we lack. Psychologically, jealousy triggers the brain's threat response, activating the same areas associated with pain and survival instincts. This is why jealousy can feel overwhelming, hijacks our emotions and creates an urgent sense of needing to protect what we believe is at risk.

It creeps in quietly because it often starts as a comparison—an innocent glance at what someone else has, a subtle feeling of not measuring up. But left unchecked, it snowballs, turning into resentment, self-doubt, or even destructive behavior. The more we feed it, the stronger it grows, shaping our perceptions and decisions in ways we don't always recognize until it has taken complete hold.

However, jealousy isn't inherently bad. It's a signal that we feel unfulfilled or insecure. When we recognize it for what it is, we shift our perspective, using it as an opportunity for self-awareness and growth rather than letting it control us.

Jealousy played a huge role in my upbringing, but it wasn't until I explored these questions that I could finally acknowledge jealousy for what it is, actively start to address it, and rid my life of its impact.

As hard as it was to face, the jealousy I grew up witnessing left a deep imprint on me—one that I unconsciously mirrored in my own behavior.

Growing up in a Hispanic household in a culture where infidelity was normalized shaped the way I viewed love and trust. From a young age, I was exposed to *telenovelas* (soap operas) where cheating wasn't just a plot point—it was glamorized. Affairs were painted with a sheen of drama and allure, characters sneaking around in passionate trysts while audiences rooted for them, even when their actions tore families apart. It created this subconscious narrative that infidelity was almost inevitable, something to be accepted rather than condemned.

In my own family, infidelity wasn't an uncommon or shocking revelation—it was an open secret. I grew up watching uncles who strayed, a grandfather who had his share of infidelities, and a father whose indiscretions planted the seeds of distrust in me long before I understood their weight. The women in my life, the matriarchs holding our families together, had been conditioned to turn a blind eye. They were taught that to keep the peace and the family intact, they had to quietly endure betrayal. In our culture, a woman's strength was measured by how much she could endure, how well she could hide her pain, and how effortlessly she could pretend everything was fine.

How do you grow up trusting anyone when the very men meant to embody loyalty and integrity betray it? And what lesson do you take from the women you admire when they quietly swallow their pain? Trust, for me, became a fragile concept. I believed love always came with a catch, and that no matter how much someone promised to be faithful, the chance of betrayal lingered in the background like an uninvited guest.

It's no wonder that this upbringing left me questioning the very foundation of relationships. I had to unlearn so much of what I was shown to rewrite the narrative that was ingrained in me. It wasn't just about learning to trust others—it was about relearning what healthy love looked like without the weight of generational wounds and the silent expectation that infidelity was just something I had to live with. After uncovering all the indiscretions within my family, I vowed never to fully depend on a man. That was the moment my armor solidified—the moment I shut my heart off from the world.

An Analysis of Jealousy

Jealousy is much far more toxic than envy. Envy is the desire to have what others have, but jealousy is rooted in fear—the fear that someone will take what is yours. It's the fear that you will be abandoned, not be good enough, or lose someone or something you treasure. It's about the fear of losing someone or something to which we've attached a significant part of our identity and sense of worth in the world.

This fear often manifests as an increased fear of potential threats to what we hold near and dear to our hearts. It's a complex emotion, often intertwined with feelings of uncertainty and inadequacy. Jealousy can appear in various forms—like admiring and longing for someone else's achievements (which leans more toward envy), feeling suspicious in romantic relationships, or displaying competitive behavior with peers. At its core, though, jealousy is limiting. It fuels the belief that you must prove yourself or become someone else to deserve what you hold dear. It keeps you constantly armored, convinced that if you let your guard down, you'll lose what matters most.

Jealousy thrives in the absence of healthy self-esteem, self-acceptance, and self-compassion. As we delve deeper into the roots of jealousy, we'll see that these factors stem from a single source: the absence of unconditional love, whether we love ourselves or others.

Fear Rooted in the Absence of Trust

Jealousy often has its roots in a deep lack of trust, whether in others or in ourselves.

When we struggle to trust those around us, we become preoccupied with fears of betrayal, deception, or loss. This constant state of worry keeps us on high alert, always searching for signs of disloyalty or dishonesty. Ironically, this fixation on proving our fears right only increases the likelihood of manifesting what we dread most.

The Law of Attraction tells us we attract more of whatever we focus on. So, the more you fixate on signs of deception, threats, or the fear of losing someone or something, the more you're drawing those very things into your energy field and turning them into your reality.

For instance, the underlying fear of being hurt or abandoned creates a suspicion cycle that strains our relationships and disrupts our peace. At its core, jealousy is fueled by this insecurity, trapping us in a state of anxiety and emotional unrest.

A lack of self-esteem plays a significant role in fueling these feelings. When we doubt our own worth, abilities, or attractiveness, we feel inadequate, and that sense of inadequacy amplifies our jealousy.

These doubts often result from experiences of rejection, failure, or criticism, leaving emotional scars. As a result, our self-esteem suffers, and jealousy becomes a mirror of our internal struggle with self-worth. Yet we hide that vulnerability from the world, masking it behind a polished suit of armor.

Fear Rooted in the Loss of Control

Jealousy is also motivated by a need for dominance.

When we sense a threat, we instinctively want to control the circumstances or individuals involved to reduce the perceived risk.

Constantly checking your partner's phone, analyzing their every move, or needing them to check in when they're not with you are all symptoms of jealousy. Jealousy can also manifest as trying to outshine the competition, backstabbing, or spreading gossip to gain an edge in the imagined contest playing out in your mind. This type of jealousy is driven by a scarcity mindset, making you feel vulnerable. So, what do you do? You armor up. But these actions are nothing more than desperate attempts to gain control, revealing just how unhealthy that state of mind truly is.

No matter how hard we try, we can't control the actions of others or dictate the outcome of every situation. The more we struggle to maintain control, the more our frustration and anxiety grows, feeding the relentless cycle of jealousy.

Fear Rooted in Insecurity

Jealousy can be rooted in insecurity, stemming from a lack of courage to be vulnerable.

This can happen when you don't see yourself being as good enough. You doubt your worth and don't believe you deserve the person or thing you're so afraid of losing. Sometimes, this fear of being exposed—often manifesting as imposter syndrome—heightens your anxiety. Deep down, a part of you feels undeserving of what you have, which fuels your insecurity.

It's a debilitating state, a life consumed by constant fear. But it goes deeper than that. This relentless fear eats away at the small sense of certainty you have left, pulling you into a downward spiral of insecurity. It leaves you feeling so fragile, so hollow, that the only thing holding you up is the armor you've built to keep from falling apart.

The Consequences of Jealousy

Jealousy is detrimental to our relationships. It can create feelings of animosity, distrust, and conflict. In love relationships, jealousy may result in possessive behavior, making allegations, and creating emotional distance. In friendships and professional environments, it can foster competition, resentment, and an absence of cooperation.

Constantly measuring ourselves against others and fearing their success slowly chips away at our own happiness. We become trapped in a relentless cycle of negativity, burdened by the belief that we continually fall short of expectations.

Being in a state of persistent jealousy makes it impossible to let down your shield and be vulnerable, keeping you trapped in a stifling state.

Escaping the Grip of Jealousy

Holding onto persistent jealousy only works against you, keeping you stuck instead of moving forward.

Employ Self-Awareness

For most of the day, many of us operate on autopilot. It's convenient, isn't it? As long as we're mentally time-traveling—either stuck ruminating on the past or anxiously worrying about the future—everything in the present runs on autopilot without our active involvement. It's not exactly living life to the fullest, but we manage.

The problem is, when we're not fully present, our defenses are down. Triggers slip past our autopilot, hijacking our emotions and throwing us into chaos before we even realize what's happening.

Self-awareness is the first and most crucial step in overcoming jealousy. It means recognizing its presence, understanding its grip on your life, and pinpointing the triggers that ignite it. In our fast-paced world, finding moments of stillness isn't easy, but those pauses are where true awareness begins. When you step away from the constant noise and turn inward, you create space to uncover the insecurities fueling these emotions—allowing yourself the power to transform them.

Practice Gratitude

Gratitude can shift your focus from what you feel you lack to the abundance already present in your life. Take a moment to appreciate the positive qualities in your relationships and wholeheartedly celebrate the successes of others. This practice deepens your connections and fosters a mindset of abundance. After all, envy and gratitude can't coexist. Over time, cultivating gratitude helps to diminish feelings of jealousy, reinforcing the belief that you're enough and that someone else's success doesn't diminish your own.

Establish Strong Boundaries

Establish clear boundaries that protect your well-being while respecting the freedom and autonomy of others. Setting boundaries means recognizing and honoring your own needs and limitations rather than trying to control or influence the behavior of those around you.

Boundaries are about letting life in on your own terms. They give you control over how you decide to interact with others and help you decide who and what you welcome into your space. It's an act of self-respect that preserves your emotional and mental well-being.

When communicating your boundaries, be both clear and compassionate, expressing your limits in a way that fosters understanding and mutual respect. This approach safeguards your well-being and promotes healthier, more balanced relationships.

Improve Communication

Open communication is essential in all relationships, whether with romantic partners, family, friends, or colleagues. Express your feelings without placing blame or making accusations. Share your desires and anxieties openly and work together to find solutions. Trust is built through honesty, openness, and a shared understanding.

Let Go of the Need for Control

Release the urge to micromanage or control others. Trust that you have the strength and resilience to overcome anything, no matter what happens. Like surrendering, letting go might feel like giving up, but it's a bold step toward confident vulnerability. Since letting go is such a crucial part of this journey, I'll explore it in greater depth in a later chapter.

Getting Practical with Reflective Prompts

Although jealousy is a natural human emotion, it doesn't have to dominate our lives. By understanding its roots, we can take proactive steps to overcome it. Building self-confidence, enhancing communication skills, letting go of the need to control others, and focusing on all the good in life are powerful strategies for transforming jealousy into a catalyst for personal growth.

The more you engage in introspection, the easier it becomes to stay present and aware of your inner landscape. Use the following prompts to dive deeper into your feelings of jealousy. Dissecting your thoughts in writing will further assist you in breaking free from jealousy's grip.

1. Think back to a recent moment when jealousy crept in. What underlying fear or insecurity did it bring to light? Instead of just reacting to the surface emotion, dig deep to address the root cause and create a meaningful shift?

2. Think back to a time when jealousy pushed you to control someone's actions or manipulate an outcome. How did that need to control impact you and your relationship? Imagine what might change if you allow yourself to let go and trust the process instead.

3. Think of someone whose success has stirred feelings of inadequacy within you. What can this situation teach you about your own aspirations and insecurities? Instead of letting envy take hold, how can you reframe their accomplishments as inspiration—proof of what's possible for you? Use their success as fuel to push yourself forward, turning comparison into motivation for your own growth.

Consult a Professional

Although mental health has gained more recognition over the years, there remains a lingering stigma around seeking professional help—especially in certain communities and cultures. The resistance toward getting professional help is rooted in the belief that it's a sign of weakness. But it's not.

Seeking support from a professional—whether it's a counselor, therapist, or life coach like me—is a true sign of strength. It means you trust yourself enough to know when to ask for support. It shows confidence in recognizing that some challenges require the expertise of others. Most importantly, it shows real confidence, the kind that comes from knowing that asking for help doesn't make you less capable, it makes you stronger. Recognizing your weaknesses and seeking support isn't a sign of failure; it's a sign of growth, a willingness to learn, and a deep understanding that your value isn't diminished by what you have yet to master.

Our society is full of contradictions. We're a collective of people who will call the cable man to fix the cable, a plumber to fix our toilets, or even a general practitioner to fix our physical ailments, but we're hesitant when we need to address our mental health concerns. Fortunately, the narrative around mental health is shifting, with more people recognizing its importance and embracing it in a positive light.

If jealousy runs deep and significantly impacts your life, trained professionals can help you explore and resolve the underlying causes, guiding you toward healthier ways of thinking and responding.

Part II:
Breaking Down the Walls

Breaking Down My Walls

I feel as if my life has hit a wall

A gigantic wall of brick and mortar

Bricks made of pain

Mortar made out of fear

A wall that has been created by me

For I have striven for so long

To live a life of perfection

Just like I have wanted all my life

In reality, what I want

What I truly want

Is more simple and basic than perfection

I just want to live

To dance as if I am among the stars

To fly as if there were no limits

To love as if I have no more days left in me (Brosevelt, 2015)

Chapter 4:
Embrace the Pain of
Transformation

"The very cave you are afraid to enter turns out to be the source of what you are looking for." – Joseph Campbell

Life is a journey of endless transformation—a process of becoming the person you're meant to be. Like a caterpillar undergoing metamorphosis, we all go through phases of profound change that shape how we see ourselves, live, and engage with the world. The key is learning to embrace these shifts, to honor the growth, the pain, the beauty, and the infinite possibilities they bring. This is how we evolve and step into the fullness of who we're meant to be.

Finding yourself in a "dark night of the soul" (more on this in Chapter 10) means you've fallen into an intense phase of inner turmoil, confusion, and existential questioning where you feel disconnected from your sense of self, purpose, or meaning of life. In this space, you come face-to-face with the shadows of your psyche—the fears, doubts, and unresolved traumas buried deep within. It's a time of intense struggle, where the very foundation of your identity feels like it's crumbling, and the ego—the part of you tied to external validation, roles, and accomplishments—begins to dissolve.

This process can feel like an overwhelming descent into chaos, where the life you once knew appears to be slipping through your fingers, leaving you feeling lost and empty. The foundations you once relied on—relationships, beliefs, ambitions—suddenly feel hollow, as if stripped of meaning, forcing you to navigate an unfamiliar path without a clear sense of direction. Yet, within this darkness, the seeds of transformation are quietly being sown. The ego, with all its illusions and attachments, begins to fade, making space for a deeper, more authentic version of yourself to emerge.

Going through a dark night feels like an ego death—a profound shedding of the false self-shaped by societal expectations, past experiences, and deeply ingrained conditioning. But this isn't a loss; it's a necessary purging of what no longer serves your highest good. It's a rite of passage into a more authentic version of yourself, where you're no longer defined by superficial measures of success or the need for external validation.

When you finally emerge from the dark night, it's as if you've been reborn—a phoenix rising from the ashes of your former self. This rebirth isn't a return to the life you once knew but a transformation into something far greater. The scars of your journey remain, but they're not signs of weakness; they're symbols of your growth and resilience. You've faced the darkest parts of yourself, and in doing so, you've come out stronger, with a profound understanding of who you truly are.

In this new state of being, you're more grounded, more connected to your intuition, and more compassionate towards yourself and others. The trials of the dark night have stripped away what no longer resonates with your soul, leaving behind unwavering strength and authenticity. You're no longer the person you once were—driven by ego and the need for validation. Instead, you're aligned with your essence, empowered by the understanding that you can endure, transform, and rise above even the greatest challenges. This metamorphosis—the reconnection with your inner light—is a hidden gift of the dark night of the soul. It's the rebirth of a stronger, wiser, and more resilient version of you, shaped by everything you've had to face and overcome.

Suffering, especially during a dark night of the soul, forces us to face the illusions created by the ego. It's painful, yes, but it's also necessary for inner transformation. Through this process, we strip away the layers of who we thought we were and discover a clearer sense of ourselves. Only then can we free ourselves from the limitations of our ego and step into the person we were always meant to be.

The Stages of Personal Metamorphosis

We admire butterflies for their delicate wings and effortless grace as they dance from flower to flower. But we rarely stop to consider the journey that led them here. Before they emerged in all their beauty and freedom, they endured a quiet, grueling transformation—one that often goes unnoticed.

A butterfly's journey is far more complex than the fleeting beauty we admire. It begins as a tiny egg, spending just 3-5 days in this delicate state before transforming into a larva, where it will spend the next 11-18 days dedicated solely to growth and survival. Then comes the most intense stage—8-14 days within the chrysalis, a period of complete transformation where it dissolves and rebuilds itself into something entirely new. All this effort and transformation, just to emerge as an adult butterfly, free and radiant, for a brief two weeks. The life we celebrate—the effortless flight, the vibrant wings—is merely the final chapter of a journey defined by patience, struggle, and an unseen metamorphosis.

By the time I turned 30, I had to let go of so many expectations I had for myself. It's tough and disheartening when your hopes, dreams, and desires don't materialize as quickly as you'd imagined. The life cycle of a butterfly is a powerful reminder that the most beautiful transformations take time. Embrace the journey, trusting that every stage has its purpose. While planning provides direction, leave room for life's surprises—sometimes, the unexpected leads to the most extraordinary growth. And through it all, be patient, be open, and most importantly, be kind to yourself.

Life is about the journey, not the destination.

The Caterpillar Stage – Living in Comfort

The caterpillar stage represents the initial phase of our existence, where we live within the boundaries of our current understanding and comfort zones. Life might feel okay during this time, but there's often a quiet yearning for more—a desire for growth, transformation, and a deeper sense of fulfillment.

The Chrysalis Stage—Embracing Transformation

The chrysalis stage is a period of profound internal transformation. It's a time of introspection, during which we confront our fears, shed old identities, and prepare for a new way of being. This stage can be challenging, as it involves letting go of the familiar and embracing the unknown.

The Butterfly Stage – Emerging in Fullness

The butterfly stage represents the unveiling of your transformed self. It's a time of renewal and growth, where you step into your full potential and live in harmony with your purpose. This stage embodies freedom, authenticity, and a profound sense of fulfillment.

Getting Practical on Your Transformation

- Are there areas in your life where you feel a deep desire for change?

- What aspects of your life feel limited or unfulfilling?

- What old beliefs, habits, or identities do you need to let go of to create space for growth?

- How can you embrace this period of transformation with courage and grace?

- How can you step into this transformation, embodying your essence and living a life of purpose and authenticity?

The Silva Method

Transformation becomes much easier when your entire being aligns with the change you seek. The Silva Method, developed by *José Silva*, a researcher in mind empowerment and human potential, and later popularized by *Mindvalley*, is designed to help you tap into the alpha brain state—a state where healing, growth, and transformation unfold with greater ease.

For most of our waking hours, our brains operate in the **beta state**, associated with active thinking, problem-solving, and alertness. However, in the moments just after waking and before falling asleep, the brain naturally transitions into the **alpha state**—a more relaxed and receptive mode linked to creativity, reduced stress, and heightened intuition. Research suggests that practices promoting alpha wave activity, such as meditation and visualization, can support emotional well-being, improve focus, and enhance overall mental clarity. While the alpha state is not a direct cure for physical ailments, it plays a crucial role in relaxation and stress reduction, which are essential factors in the body's natural healing process.

The Silva Method provides a structured approach to accessing the alpha state at will, rather than relying on natural sleep cycles. With simple yet effective techniques, it allows you to harness the full potential of your mind, leading to enhanced self-awareness, emotional balance, and personal growth. Best of all, with consistent practice, this method can unlock profound mental and emotional benefits in as little as 40 days.

Getting Practical with The Silva Method

When you awake, resist the urge to grab your phone. Give yourself a moment to stay disconnected. If you need to use the bathroom, do so quickly, then return to bed, sit upright, and relax.

Close your eyes and begin counting backward from 100 to 0 in your mind. Repeat this practice every morning for 10 days. Then, for the next 10 days, count from 50 to 0. After that, reduce it to 25 to 0, and finally, for the last phase, count from 10 to 0 each morning.

By doing this, you're training your brain to slip into the alpha state at will—helping you access clarity, creativity, and calm throughout your day. Once you've conditioned yourself, you'll be able to count down from 10 to 0 anytime and instantly shift into this state, using it to release limiting beliefs, reconnect with your inner child (more on that in Chapter Six), and create meaningful change in your life.

In this state, your intuition is heightened, and manifestation becomes effortless allowing you to align with what you desire.

Embracing the Pain and Beauty of Transformation

Change isn't just uncomfortable—it's disruptive. It shakes the foundation of who you thought you were, forcing you to question everything you once believed. It unravels your certainties, exposing the cracks in the identity you've spent years constructing. No wonder it's tempting to resist. No wonder we cling to what's familiar, even when it no longer serves us.

But here's the truth: at some point, staying the same becomes unbearable. The weight of stagnation grows heavier than the fear of the unknown. You reach a moment when the life you've outgrown starts to choke you, and suddenly, the pain of transformation feels like the only way forward.

This is where the magic happens, on the other side of that fear— beyond the discomfort, the doubt, the moments you want to turn back remind yourself of awakes. A version of you that is no longer weighed down by old wounds, outdated narratives, or your past. Yes, growth is messy. Yes, it requires you to shed layers you once thought you couldn't live without. But what if everything you've ever wanted is waiting for you on the other side of this discomfort? What if who you're becoming is worth the temporary pain?

The Power of Surrender

One of the most powerful aspects of metamorphosis is the act of surrender. Just as the caterpillar surrenders to the process of transformation within the chrysalis, we, too, must surrender to the natural flow of our personal evolution.

This surrender is about trusting the process and allowing ourselves to be guided by a deeper wisdom. It's about trusting in our resilience and believing in our ability to handle and overcome whatever challenges come our way. It's an act of bravery that demands vulnerability.

Surrendering means releasing the need to control every detail of your life and trusting that every experience—no matter how challenging—is shaping you into who you're meant to be. It's about embracing uncertainty with faith, knowing that transformation isn't about loss, but about alignment. On the other side of letting go lies a more authentic, empowered version of you, waiting to emerge.

Getting Practical with Your Metamorphosis

"I am not what happened to me; I am what I choose to become." – Carl Jung

You can transform, shape your journey, and choose when to enter your next growth and evolution stage.

Carl Jung, the renowned Swiss psychiatrist and founder of analytical psychology, taught that we are not prisoners of our past—our future is shaped by our willingness to grow and evolve. His wisdom reminds us that life isn't defined by what happened yesterday, but by the choices we make today. The present moment holds the power to rewrite our story, allowing us to step into a future guided by intention rather than limitation.

As you navigate your own metamorphosis, remember that each stage is necessary and valuable. Trust the process, surrender to the flow, and embrace the path with an open heart. You will emerge stronger, wiser, and more aligned with your true self, ready to soar to new heights.

This metamorphosis of your existence invites you to step into your potential and live a life of meaning, purpose, and authenticity. Embrace the journey, and watch your life unfold in unexpected ways.

Chapter 5:
What We Hold Onto, Holds Us Back

We all carry things that weigh us down—memories, expectations, and beliefs buried beneath years of habits and reactions. We cling to them tightly, convinced they define us, protect us, or shape who we are.

It's the things we refuse to let go of that keep our armor intact.

As we navigate life, we often carry emotional baggage—regrets from the past and unmet expectations that weigh us down.

Who or What Are You Blaming?

It's easy to point fingers at others when life doesn't go as we planned. Children often grow up hearing their parents blame the government when money is tight or their employers when they feel unfulfilled at work. While there may be some truth in these complaints, the habit of blaming doesn't usually stop there.

Reflect on a time when you felt the weight of a particular event or circumstance from your past. Perhaps it was a mistake, a failed relationship, or a missed opportunity. Often filled with regret and sadness, these memories can weigh heavy on your heart and mind, holding you back and slowing down your progress.

Carrying this weight through life wears you down by making every step feel harder, and your goals seem farther away. Progress becomes a struggle, and genuine happiness feels out of reach. To reach your full potential and find real joy, you must let go of the burdens you've been carrying.

For years, I clung to my stories, my pain, and my fears. They became my armor and the shield I thought would protect me.

I had it all wrong. Letting go isn't about losing yourself; it's about liberating yourself to become something greater, and clearing space to evolve into the person you were always meant to be.

Growing up, I watched my parents hold onto their pain as if letting go meant losing a piece of themselves. I get it now. There's a strange comfort in misery, a sense of familiarity that makes staying stuck feel safer than changing. Without realizing it, parents pass down this mindset to their children, conditioning them to seek external blame rather than looking within. This cycle has likely played out for generations—through your parents, and now through you—unless you decide to break it. Staying in the familiar feels safe, even when it's slowly eroding who you are. You hold onto old identities, even as they weigh you down, until one day, you barely recognize yourself. Misery, self-doubt, and the feeling of not being enough seep into your sense of self, embedding so deeply that they start to feel like a core part of who you are. Letting go of these views isn't just uncomfortable—it can feel like losing a piece of yourself. But in truth, it's not loss; it's liberation.

My parents didn't talk much about the hard times, but you could feel it—in the air, how they carried themselves, and how they went through life. Although the hard times didn't stop them from moving forward, they did cast a shadow over our household. It was like living in perpetual twilight, and never quite stepping into the full light of life. Their unspoken rule was to keep going but never to forget where they came from. They held onto their scars like prized possessions, reminders of lessons learned and pain they vowed never to repeat.

I inherited that belief. Like them, I thought that holding onto every memory would protect me, that if I never forgot, I could never be hurt the same way twice. But that's the trap—gripping too tightly to the past only anchors you to it. Over time, it seeps into every part of you until the day you try to break free and realize you're no longer guarding yourself from pain—you're just living inside it, surrounded by the very memories you swore would keep you safe.

It reminds me of *The Lion King's* Simba, who, after the loss of his father, runs away and builds a life far from his past. For years, he avoids his pain, convincing himself that forgetting is the best way to move forward. But despite his new life, there's always something missing—his identity, his purpose, his rightful place in the world. It isn't until he faces his past, rather than running from it or holding onto it with resentment, that he's able to step into the life he was meant for.

Like Simba, I had to learn that real strength isn't in running from the past or gripping onto it for dear life—it's in making peace with it. It's in allowing yourself to acknowledge what shaped you without letting it define you. Because the past isn't meant to be a home—it's meant to be a lesson. And when you finally learn that, you step into something greater: freedom.

The Illusion of Control

We often believe we have more control or influence over a situation than we do.

This illusion of control is one of the biggest hurdles to overcome. We hold on tightly to people, outcomes, and emotions, believing our grip can influence or change them. Complete control is an illusion. Life is unpredictable by its very nature, and our efforts to dominate it often leads to frustration and disappointment.

Letting go means embracing the reality that some things are beyond our control. In this acceptance, we find peace and open ourselves up to greater possibilities.

The first time I let go in a big way was when I was in my first serious relationship. The relationship was filled with many ups and downs (as most relationships are), and despite all the red flags, I kept clinging on. I convinced myself that if I just worked hard enough, I could make it work. I held on tightly, driven by fear of failure, fear of the pain that comes from letting go, and fear of what it might say about me if I couldn't hold it all together.

I thought I was going to marry him—everyone did. Our friends, our families, everyone who knew us thought so too. But I will never forget the moment he said, "You don't love me." I pushed back. *What do you mean? Of course, I love you.* I said it with conviction, believing it to be true. But something about his words lingered, unsettling me in a way I couldn't explain. It wasn't until much later that I finally admitted the truth to myself: he was right. I didn't love him. Not because I didn't care, but because I couldn't let him in.

How could I? I didn't even believe I was lovable myself. I kept a safe distance—not consciously, but in ways he could feel. That's the thing about energy; it never lies. I thought love was about showing up, being present, and doing the right things. But love is also about openness, about allowing someone to see you. And I couldn't do that. I had spent so much of my life protecting myself that I never realized just how emotionally unavailable I was.

And then, during one of our last fights, right before our breakup, I blurted out, "I can't believe you're going to make me start dating in my 30s." The second those words left my mouth, it hit me—I was in this relationship for all the wrong reasons. I wasn't staying because I loved him; I was staying because I was afraid. Afraid to start over. Afraid of being alone. I was afraid to admit that I had never truly loved him the way I knew, deep in my soul, I was capable of loving.

Like so many painful endings, that breakup became the turning point for my spiritual awakening. I'd hit rock bottom, walking through my own dark night of the soul. And in that darkness, I realized something profound: I had to change if I ever wanted to be happy. I had to return to myself, to my wholeness, and let go of everything that was holding me back from the life I wanted. I saw how much of myself had been lost in that relationship—how it drained me, I became a shell of the person I once was.

For years, I had been drawn to emotionally unavailable men, unaware that I was mirroring the very thing I feared most— disconnection. I told myself I wanted depth, vulnerability, real intimacy, but I kept choosing partners who couldn't offer it. And the truth was, I wasn't offering it either. I kept them at arm's length, afraid to let them in, afraid of being seen too clearly. Even in the relationships that seemed promising, I never fully opened. It was safer that way. But safety wasn't love, it was survival. And survival mode had been my default setting for far too long.

I heard Dr. Gabor Maté say the words *health* and *wholeness* are derived from the same Anglo-Saxon word. That made sense to me. We need to be whole to be healthy, and my desire to control everything was making me sick mentally, emotionally, and physically. Eventually, I hit a breaking point, realizing I had two choices: keep holding on to something that wasn't serving me, or let go and step into my power.

Letting go felt like a freefall. It usually does. I had spent so long wrapped up in that relationship that I no longer knew who I was without it. And the thought of figuring that out, especially at that point of my life, was nothing short of terrifying. But the moment I let go, I felt an unexpected relief—a lightness I hadn't felt in years. It was as if all the energy I'd spent holding on was suddenly available to me again. That moment showed me that letting go isn't about giving up. Instead, it's a choice to no longer be weighed down by past events or things that no longer serve you. It's freeing yourself to embrace the present and open yourself to the future you deserve.

Letting go wasn't easy—it took constant effort and intentional action. But it all began with a single decision: to set myself free. It's about making a conscious choice to release what no longer serves you—the habits, relationships, and beliefs that keep you stuck. True freedom comes when you create space for what matters, unburdened by the weight of what you were never meant to carry.

The first step in letting go is identifying what you're holding onto and understanding why. Sometimes we're aware of what's weighing us down. Other times, these burdens are so deeply ingrained that we barely notice them. They become like background noise, quietly humming in our minds, shaping our decisions and how we see ourselves without us even realizing it.

Practical Steps to Identify What to Let Go

Set aside time to reflect on your life. Choose a quiet space where you won't be interrupted and take a few deep breaths to center yourself and settle into a calm state.

- Let your mind wander as you reflect on your beliefs about success, relationships, well-being, wealth, and happiness. Ask yourself: Are these beliefs empowering and aligned with what you want in life, or are they limiting you and keeping you from achieving desired abundance?

- Take a moment to identify the toxic people in your life, the ones who leave you feeling drained or emotionally empty whenever you're around them. Reflect on the beliefs that keep you tied to these relationships. What stories are you telling yourself that make it hard to let go?

- Reflect on the most dramatic or painful events from your past. How much space do they still occupy in your mind? Do they continue to influence your decisions today? Consider what opportunities or experiences you may have missed because you've allowed these moments to shape the course of your life.

- Pay attention to how often your mind focuses on the things you desire. Do these thoughts leave you feeling a sense of lack and frustration, or do they inspire and motivate you to act toward your goals?

Letting Go of the Need to Be Perfect

Growing up, I always felt a pressure to be "good"—to do everything right, avoid mistakes, and meet both the spoken and unspoken expectations placed on me. Somewhere along the line, I internalized the belief that my worth was tied to my performance. It became part of my identity, driving me to overwork, over-please, and second-guess myself endlessly. It wasn't until I hit complete burnout that I realized my perfectionism wasn't pushing me forward—it was holding me back. I wasn't living my life; I was simply performing.

In the best-seller *Daring Greatly: How the Courage to be Vulnerable Transforms the Way We Live, Love, Parent, and Lead*, Brené Brown explains that perfectionism doesn't bring anyone joy. In fact, the persistent drive to achieve an impossible outcome steals your joy and leaves you feeling depleted, demotivated, and depressed. She adds that despite people perceiving perfectionism as a route to excellence, self-improvement, achievement, or escaping shame, this is inaccurate. According to Brené, perfectionism is an addictive, self-destructive habit robbing life of fullness and the beauty found in imperfection.

Piece by piece, I started letting go of my need for perfection. It didn't happen all at once—it was a slow, often frustrating process. There were moments when I slipped back into old habits— rewriting emails multiple times to make them sound just right, overanalyzing every word before posting on social media, or feeling paralyzed by the fear of making a mistake in front of others. If something wasn't flawless, I convinced myself it wasn't worth sharing. But in chasing perfection, I was only holding myself back.

But each time I caught myself slipping into perfectionism, I reminded myself that my worth isn't something I have to earn—it's inherent. I allowed myself to send that email without over-analyzing, to post the picture even if it wasn't perfect, and to speak up in meetings even if I didn't have the most polished response. Letting go of perfection didn't make me lazy or careless; it allowed me to be free. It gave me the space to focus on what mattered to me—connection, creativity, and growth—rather than chasing an unattainable standard that was never mine to begin with.

Self-compassion is the antidote to perfectionism—the key to embracing life's imperfections rather than resisting them. Mark Manson, bestselling author of The Subtle Art of Not Giving a F*ck, emphasizes that "the desire for more positive experience is itself a negative experience. And, paradoxically, the acceptance of one's negative experience is itself a positive experience." His words highlight a fundamental truth: constantly striving for perfection only creates more dissatisfaction, while true growth comes from accepting ourselves—flaws and all. When we let go of the pressure to be flawless and replace self-judgment with self-compassion, we open the door to greater fulfillment, resilience, and personal freedom.

Practical Steps to Let Go of Perfection

Cultivating self-compassion naturally eases the grip of perfectionism, allowing it to fade gradually from your life. However, self-compassion isn't a one time achievement—it's an ongoing practice, a commitment to freeing yourself from the relentless pressure of perfection.

- Take a moment to reflect on something you've been criticizing yourself for. Now, shift your perspective and speak to yourself the way you'd speak to your best friend. What would you say to comfort or encourage them? How would you motivate them with kindness and understanding? When you use those same words to uplift yourself, you give yourself the same compassion.

- What feels challenging or difficult to accept about the situation you're facing? And on the other hand, what unexpected beauty or opportunity might be found within it?

We all have a choice—hide what we perceive as flaws or embrace them as part of what makes us uniquely beautiful. Which path will you take?

Letting Go of Resentment

Resentment is one of the heaviest burdens we can carry. For years, I held onto anger toward those I believed had wronged me, convincing myself it was a form of self-protection.

My resentment didn't hurt the people I resented. Most of them moved on with their lives, completely unaffected, while I remained stuck, weighed down by bitterness and pain. As the saying goes, *"Resentment is like drinking poison and expecting the other person to die."* In the end, the only person it destroys is the one holding onto it.

I spent far too long trapped in that bitterness, thinking it would shield me from ever being hurt again. But all it did was keep me bound to the very patterns I was trying to break free from. By holding onto resentment, I relived old wounds, keeping them raw and open instead of allowing them to heal.

I resisted forgiveness for a long time, believing it meant letting others off the hook, giving them a pass for hurting me, but I eventually realized that forgiveness is about freeing yourself from the hold of the past. When I chose to forgive, I wasn't condoning the hurt; I was choosing to stop letting it define me. I was choosing peace.

Self-forgiveness is even harder. I carried the weight of regret for my actions, choices, and words I couldn't take back. I replayed those moments over and over, wishing I could turn back time and make different choices.

Nurture Acceptance

Forgiveness leads us to acceptance, even when it feels nearly impossible to accept those who appear indifferent to our needs, values, or sense of right and wrong. Thankfully, acceptance becomes more natural when you open your mind and allow your soul to guide you. Spirit offers wisdom and perspective, helping you let go of resistance and embrace a more compassionate understanding of others and the world around you.

When you accept the world as it is and people for who they are without expecting them to give you what they simply cannot, life becomes far less burdensome. The weight of disappointment lifts, and the constant need to keep your emotional armor intact fades away.

Getting Practical on Forgiveness

Holding onto regret serves no one—it only stunts your growth. I learned to forgive myself by recognizing that I did my best with the tools I had now. Self-forgiveness allowed me to see my mistakes not as permanent flaws but as valuable lessons that helped shape who I am today.

- Are you ready to forgive others or yourself and step into your freedom?

- Who or what do you need to forgive?

- What emotions are tied to this event or experience?

- What steps can you take now to address or make amends for what happened?

- Have you taken those steps?

- What lessons have you gained from this experience?

- How can you use this lesson to grow and benefit your future?

Imagine how your life could transform if you let go of this burden. Reflect on what you must accept about the situation to make genuine forgiveness possible. Once you've spent time sitting with the idea of forgiveness, try shifting your focus to the good that came from the experience—no matter how small. It could be anything, even something as simple as realizing the lessons you learned or the strength you gained along the way. Now consider how it would feel if someone who needs to forgive you took this same compassionate approach.

The Power of Facing Uncertainty with an Open Heart

I had to let go of the expectation that I'd have it all figured out by my 30s, but here I am. My life now feels like the famous line from *Forrest Gump* when Tom Hanks says, "Life is like a box of chocolates—you never know what you're going to get." It may not be what I envisioned, but it's been an incredible journey. With all its highs and lows, this journey has shaped me and prepared me for everything yet to come. These days, I've stopped obsessing over where I "should" be and started embracing where I am. Instead of rigidly clinging to a plan, I focus on living and savoring each day, knowing that the detours, surprises, and unexpected turns are all part of the adventure. Letting go of those old expectations hasn't been easy, but it has transformed my perspective—and in doing so, it has transformed me.

We can plan our lives all we want, but life has a funny way of surprising us.

I remember the first time I noticed this shift. I was home meditating; I suddenly felt a profound sense of peace. I stopped judging myself; I stopped replaying old stories, and I wasn't bracing myself for the next challenge. I was simply there, present, open. It was a small incident, but it was very powerful. It reminded me that life doesn't have to be a constant struggle. Letting go also means stepping into the unknown. It requires surrendering control, accepting that we don't have all the answers, and trusting that life will unfold as it's meant to. For someone like me—who spent years trying to control every outcome—that was terrifying. But I've learned that true freedom lies in releasing the need to have everything figured out and embracing the adventure of uncertainty. The unknown, just beyond the edges of your comfort zone, is where life begins. It's where we uncover who we really are—beyond our roles, beyond our expectations, and beyond the stories we tell ourselves. By releasing the need for control, I learned to trust myself, trust the process, and embrace the truth that I'm enough exactly where I belong. Letting go taught me that strength is knowing when to release. The strength I once thought came from control, from walls and defenses, I now find in kindness, vulnerability, and honesty. By letting go, I found a kind of resilience that doesn't need armor; it only requires trust.

Getting Practical in Letting Go

1. Before you can let go, you must acknowledge how you feel. Emotions can be elusive. When you deny them, they tend to push harder for your attention. Instead, allow yourself to fully experience the pain, anger, or grief without attaching judgment or criticism. Embracing your emotions with compassion and without judgment is a vital step in healing, creating space for growth.

2. Every experience, no matter how painful, carries a valuable lesson. Take a moment to reflect on what you've learned from the situation. How has it contributed to your personal growth? What wisdom or insights have you gained that you can carry forward and apply to the future?

3. Give yourself the space to release your emotions in a healthy and constructive way. Explore different avenues to express your thoughts and feelings openly. Write them down, share them with a trusted friend, or channel them into creative outlets like painting, music, or any form of art that resonates with you. This act of expression helps to release the emotional energy tied to past experiences, paving the way for healing.

4. Practice mindfulness to anchor yourself in the present moment. Activities like meditation, deep breathing exercises, or yoga can help quiet your mind, center your thoughts, and release the hold of past experiences. These practices allow you to focus on the here and now, fostering a sense of peace and clarity.

5. Recognize that change is an inevitable part of life and choose to embrace it with an open mind and heart. While change is often seen as negative, it holds just as much potential to cultivate positivity and growth. Every ending paves the way for a new beginning, and every loss creates space for fresh opportunities to emerge.

6. Creating new routines can break the cycle of old habits and thought patterns, opening the door to fresh perspectives and growth. Seek out activities that bring you genuine joy and a deep sense of fulfillment and make them a regular part of your daily life.

Letting go is a journey. Each step reveals a deeper sense of freedom and inner strength. You'll come to realize that your identity isn't defined by your past but by the choices you make in the present moment.

Chapter 6:
Heal Your Inner Child, Heal Your Life

We must listen to the inner child we once were, the child who still exists inside us. That child understands magic moments. We can stifle its cries, but we cannot silence it. –Paulo Coelho

When you're overwhelmed with anger and ready to respond with aggression (sometimes not even knowing why), take a step back. You're likely to see a glimpse of the hurt inner child hiding inside you.

The inner child, quietly residing beneath the surface of our adult selves, is the part of us that holds our earliest memories, emotions, and experiences. The inner child represents the part of ourselves that is innocent, vulnerable, and susceptible to being influenced by others, shaped during our tender, formative years.

Dr. Bruce Lipton, a cellular biologist, posits that early childhood experiences shape our subconscious programming, influencing our perceptions and behaviors in adulthood. He explains that from birth until about age seven, children's brains predominantly operate in a theta brainwave state—a highly receptive condition akin to hypnosis. Children absorb beliefs, behaviors, and emotional patterns from their environment during this period without critical analysis. According to Dr. Lipton, these absorbed patterns form the foundation of the subconscious mind, which governs approximately 95% of our behavior in adult life.

Rather than forcing children into a socially accepted mold, the true role of parenting lies in recognizing, embracing, and nurturing each child's unique personality. This means meeting their physical and emotional needs through acceptance, unconditional love, and quality time together. Unfortunately, some parents have strayed from this essential purpose, losing sight of what truly matters in raising confident, well-rounded children.

Like their parents and the generation before them, some parents are completely misinformed about what to expect when they become parents. This isn't due to malice or neglect but rather a gap in understanding and knowledge. When parents lack this awareness, the question arises: What impact does this have on the child?

When our needs as children weren't met, we found ways to retreat—whether into real places or imaginary worlds of our own making. I remember curling up in a hidden nook of my childhood bedroom, a book in hand, escaping into a world where I felt safe. For some, it was a treehouse, a favorite hiding spot, or even the quiet hum of a television in the background that made them feel less alone. Others found safety in creating—drawing, writing, or daydreaming about a life where they felt seen. And then there were those who withdrew inward, disconnecting from their feelings altogether to avoid disappointment or rejection. These spaces provided temporary relief, but they also reinforced the belief that it wasn't safe to be seen.

Children build walls and wear masks to protect themselves, concealing their true selves from the world. Why do we do this? Because at some point, we felt like our true selves weren't enough for the people whose love we needed the most.

For some, this meant becoming the overachiever, excelling in school or sports in hopes of earning praise. Others played the role of the peacemaker, suppressing their own emotions to keep the household calm. Some became the "strong one," learning early on that showing vulnerability led to rejection or disappointment. And then there were those who faded into the background, staying quiet and unseen, believing that being invisible was the safest way to avoid judgement and criticism.

These adaptations helped us survive our childhoods, but as adults, they become the very walls that keep us from forming meaningful connections. The overachiever fears failure, the peacemaker struggles with boundaries, the strong one hesitates to ask for help, and the invisible child wonders if their presence matters.

Recognizing these patterns is the first step toward healing. Only by understanding how we learned to protect ourselves can we begin to let down our walls, take off the masks, and embrace who we are.

A wounded inner child doesn't always come from obvious trauma—sometimes, emotional scars form in the quiet moments, in what was missing rather than what happened. The absence of inner peace becomes the inner child's home—a restless space buried deep inside us. Masks and barriers prevent healing from happening in that space.

Sometimes, life gets so tough that it cracks your mask and damages the walls you've built. But instead of breaking you, something unexpected happens. The light seeps into the darkness behind the mask, beyond the barriers you've erected. As Rumi beautifully said, "The wound is the place where the light enters you." This light reaches your wounded inner child, illuminating the pain and calling for healing.

Inner child healing allows us to reconnect with and mend the wounds of our past, fostering deeper self-awareness, emotional liberation, and a profound sense of wholeness.

Carl Jung reminded us, "In every adult, there lurks a child—an eternal child, something that is always becoming, is never completed, and calls for unceasing care, attention, and education. That is the part of the human personality which wants to develop and become whole."

Symptoms of a Wounded Inner Child

If you're constantly running on autopilot, you might overlook the subtle but important signs that your inner child is seeking your attention. Sometimes, you might even choose to ignore your inner child's cries for attention, too afraid to face what lies within. But neither avoidance nor operating on autopilot leads to inner peace.

The following are unmistakable signs of unresolved pain and anguish lingering within you.

Overreacting to the Little Things

When certain situations or interactions provoke intense emotional reactions out of proportion to the event itself, it's often a reflection of unresolved childhood wounds. Let's be honest: most people neglect introspection and avoid taking the necessary steps for personal growth and healing. As a result, it's not uncommon to witness an adult reacting in a way that mirrors the emotions of a six-year-old.

It's easy to label these actions as childish, but what's really happening is that the inner child has taken the stage. Instead of passing judgment—on someone else or yourself—recognize that this behavior stems from an unhealed childhood wound. Until these wounds are acknowledged and addressed, they'll continue to resurface in the most unexpected ways, bringing back the same overwhelming emotions you felt as a child.

Self-Sabotaging Patterns

Do you ever catch yourself stuck in the same cycles, doing the same things repeatedly, only to end up with the same miserable results? Perhaps you notice patterns in your relationships or behaviors that trace back to childhood, like a fear of rejection, abandonment issues, or always needing approval. For example, you might constantly seek validation from others or feel terrified of being left alone; these feelings are all rooted in the lack of emotional security you may have felt as a child. These patterns can keep you stuck, holding you back in your relationships, your career, and your life as a whole.

Low Self-Esteem

Feelings of inadequacy, unworthiness, or self-criticism often stem from the negative messages you absorbed during childhood. As Dr. Maté explains, every person is born whole, with an essential need for love, acceptance, and validation. When these needs go unmet—especially by a critical or emotionally unavailable parent—it can create a deeply rooted belief that you're not good enough.

Difficulty Trusting Others

Do relationships feel overwhelmingly difficult for you? Do you find yourself deeply afraid of rejection, caught in lingering tension, or emotionally dependent on others? Maybe trust feels like a constant battle, or forming close connections seems impossible because of past betrayals or abandonment. If you experienced neglect or inconsistency from your caregivers early in life, you may have internalized a deep-rooted belief that others will eventually let you down—that love, safety, and stability are always just out of reach.

Pleasing Others

You might push yourself to be perfect or go out of your way to please others, often sacrificing your needs. Perhaps you're constantly running on empty, teetering on the edge of burnout because your days are consumed with caring for everyone else, leaving no time for yourself and your needs. This behavior often stems from a childhood need to earn love or approval. For example, growing up with conditional love or being held to impossibly high standards can lead to a relentless drive for perfection in adulthood.

Steps to Ultimate Healing of Old Wounds

Inner child wounds don't just disappear. If you fail to attend to the needs of your inner child, your past will continue to haunt your present and future.

Chances are, no one intentionally meant to cause you harm. But it's your responsibility to mend those wounds. Are you willing to repeat the cycle by neglecting your inner child, or will you find the courage to step into vulnerability, take that child by the hand, and guide them toward safety and unconditional love?

Louise Hay reminds us that we all carry a child within us, yet most of the time we're unknowingly shouting at that child instead of listening to its needs. Hay emphasizes the importance of addressing the wounds within, highlighting that true freedom comes only when confronting and healing our inner child. Until then, we remain trapped in a cycle, repeating the same mistakes and repeatedly experiencing the same hurts.

Get to Know Your Inner Child

Your inner child isn't a separate part of you, it's deeply woven into every part of your being. Because this part of your identity is so vulnerable, it might feel unfamiliar or even strange to connect with. To understand your inner child, you must reconnect with what that version of yourself once felt, dreamed about, and hoped for.

Self-awareness lets you observe your inner child better and understand its needs and wants. It'll also direct you to the nature of the wounds causing your suffering.

Listen to Your Inner Child

As adults, we're so quick to jump in with solutions, advice, or answers to our problems. Instead, try to take time to just stop and listen. It's the first and most essential step before any meaningful healing can occur.

Your inner child might have unmet needs or bottled-up emotions that are begging to be acknowledged. Give them a safe space to express themselves, free from judgment. Write a letter inviting your inner child to share their thoughts and emotions. Respond with empathy and understanding, offering reassurance and love.

Reparent Yourself with Kindness

Reparenting yourself involves providing the care, guidance, and love that your inner child may not have received. This process allows you to meet your inner child's needs in a nurturing way. By listening to your inner child, you gain clarity on the wounds that shaped you and what's required to mend them. With that understanding, you can step in and be the parent your inner child has always longed for, providing the love and support they deserve.

Getting Practical in Reparenting Yourself

The more you practice mindfulness, the easier it'll become to detect moments when you feel vulnerable or triggered, before your inner child lashes out. In those moments, pause and ask yourself, "What does my inner child need right now?" Then, offer yourself some comforting words, a calming ritual, or a supportive action to help your inner child feel safe and cared for.

Play More Often

The child within each of us thrives on play. Play is a powerful way to learn and grow, regardless of age. It's essential to developing creativity, curiosity, and joy, which is vital to your inner child's well-being. Activities that spark happiness, like drawing, dancing, or playing games, can help you reconnect with your inner child's natural spontaneity and zest for life. Dedicate time each week to a playful or creative activity that you enjoyed as a child. Allow yourself to immerse in the experience.

Seek Professional Support

Inner child healing is a profound and complex journey. Sometimes, the wounds run so deep that it feels impossible to address them on your own, or you may struggle to gain the perspective needed to truly shift your mindset. In such cases, working with a professional specializing in inner child healing can provide invaluable guidance and support. They can offer tools, techniques, and a safe, compassionate space to help you navigate this extremely transformative process.

Meditate to Heal Your Inner Child

Meditation is a powerful tool for accessing a state of heightened awareness where you can release the pain your inner child has been holding onto. In this mindful state, it becomes easier to tune into your inner child's emotions and understand what they need to heal. Meditation also allows you to reshape your internal narrative, replacing negative mental chatter with positive affirmations that foster healing and growth.

Getting Practical on Meditation for Inner Child Healing

1. Find a comfortable position, close your eyes, and take a deep breath in.

2. Slowly exhale, letting go of any tension.

3. Visualize yourself as a child. See your younger self standing in front of you, innocent. Notice their expression, posture, and energy.

4. Now, imagine yourself kneeling to their level. Reach out and gently hold their hands. Feel the warmth and connection between you.

5. Speak to your inner child with love. Tell your inner child you see him or her and understand their pain, fears, and hopes. Reassure them that you're there to protect, nurture, and love you unconditionally.

6. Embrace your inner child, feeling a warm, healing light surrounding both of you. Let that light fill every corner of your being, bringing comfort and peace.

7. Take another deep breath in. As you exhale, imagine the light expanding, healing any lingering wounds, and strengthening your bond.

When you're ready, slowly open your eyes, bringing that sense of healing and love with you into the present moment.

The Moment Everything Changed

A pivotal moment in my journey of healing my inner child was tied to my upbringing. While my basic needs were met, my parents were so young—just 22 and 25 when they had me. They were still figuring out how to be happy themselves. The lack of affection and attention created a deep sense of instability and disappointment early on, shaping how I viewed relationships, trust, and love. It became difficult for me to rely on anyone, and that fear of being let down seeped into every aspect of my life.

I've always valued my privacy, but I also know that if I've faced these struggles and traumas, I must have as well. My hope in sharing my story is to offer hope and clarity to those who need it most—to remind them they're not alone and that it's okay not to have it all figured out.

I thought if I kept people at a distance, I could protect myself from being hurt. But I was wrong. I had to go back and heal that little girl who felt abandoned and unworthy of love, the one who didn't trust anyone to show up for her.

Healing my inner child meant forgiving my parents. They were wounded themselves and did the best they could with what they knew. I had to let go of the anger and sadness I carried from feeling like I wasn't enough. This healing allowed me to finally open up, trust again, and allow love into my life. Without it, I wouldn't have the peace, confidence, or strength I have today. It's what's allowed me to step into my purpose as a coach, guiding others to heal their own wounds and live more fulfilling lives.

Embarking on the journey of healing your inner child is daunting and exciting.

The more you nurture and care for your inner child, the more you uncover the essence of who you are—innocent, creative, and brimming with unlimited potential. Every time you connect with your inner child, you take a step toward transforming your relationship with yourself and opening the door to a richer, more fulfilling life.

Chapter 7:
Emotional Upgrading

For human beings, simply put, the default state is happiness. If you don't believe me, spend a little time with a human fresh from the factory, an infant or toddler. Obviously, there's a lot of crying and fussing associated with the start-up phase of little humans, but the fact is, if their most basic needs are met—no immediate hunger, no immediate fear, no scary isolation, no physical pain or enduring sleeplessness—they live in the moment, perfectly happy. –Mo Gawdat

Growing up in Brooklyn, NY, made me naturally wary of people. I was always on high alert, ready to defend myself at a moment's notice. Growing up, I was surrounded by drugs and violence in my neighborhood. The instinct to protect myself grew stronger the older I got. Trust didn't come easily for me, and relying on others never felt safe. My default setting was one of distrust and vigilance, constantly expecting to be hurt—not necessarily physically, though the streets could be rough, but more so mentally and emotionally.

Did constantly bracing for an attack make me happy? Not at all. Most of the threats I imagined never materialized, but did that bring me relief? Absolutely not. I still couldn't feel happiness or gratitude. My emotional default left me trapped in a miserable cycle, weighed down by the heavy armor I'd built around myself.

Why did I not feel happy when all the terrible things I'd visualized and protected myself against didn't come to fruition?

Egyptian entrepreneur and author Mo Gawdat of *Solve for Happy* explains that it all concerns the *Happiness Equation. The* Happiness Equation determines that your happiness equals or exceeds the difference between the events in your life and your expectations of how life should be.

It's easy to assume I should've felt happy and at peace when all the bad things I anticipated—shaped by my past experiences and perceptions—didn't happen. But because I'd conditioned myself to expect a world where I always needed to be on guard, the gap between what I expected and what actually occurred was too wide for me to find joy. Although my armor might have shielded me from vulnerability, it offered no way for happiness to enter my shell.

This brings me back to a fundamental truth: we're all born with happiness as our natural state.

In childhood, happiness is effortless, tied only to the fulfillment of basic needs. As we grow, we stray from that innate sense of joy. One day, we wake up and realize how far we've strayed from the joy that once felt so natural. By then, happiness can feel so distant, so out of reach, that finding our way back seems almost impossible.

My emotional default state changed when I stopped seeing myself as a victim and blaming others for my sadness, anger, fears, and crippling inability to be vulnerable.

Once I laid down my sword and set aside my armor, I could finally live a happier, more fulfilling life.

When my life's expectations became more realistic and aligned with what was happening, it was like a veil was lifted, and I saw people for who they truly are—wounded children in adult bodies. With that realization came a deep sense of compassion, not only for others but also for me. I stopped judging and started leading with love.

Upgrade Your Emotional Default

Do you have complete control over your emotional baseline or default state? Various scientific studies have increasingly linked our emotional baseline, or the default state of our emotional responses, to our DNA and ancestral background. Recent research in epigenetics continues to support the notion that ancestral experiences can leave genetic imprints affecting descendants' emotional and psychological health. A 2022 bibliometric analysis evaluated 1,151 publications on childhood trauma and epigenetics from 2000 to 2021, highlighting the growing interest and evidence in this field (*Frontiers in Psychiatry, 13*).

Additionally, a 2023 review focused on the intergenerational transmission of trauma effects, emphasizing the role of epigenetic mechanisms in this process (Research digest: understanding intergenerational trauma and its transmission through the lens of epigenetics. *Journal of Child Psychotherapy, 50*).

These studies underscore the significant impact of ancestral experiences on the well-being of subsequent generations.

This means we all have a specific emotional DNA.

For instance, a study conducted by researchers at Emory University found that mice trained to fear a specific smell passed on this learned fear to their offspring, demonstrating that traumatic experiences can affect the DNA in the sperm or egg and alter the brains and behavior of subsequent generations (*Mice Can Inherit Learned Sensitivity to Smell*, 2014). Similarly, human studies have indicated that children and grandchildren of Holocaust survivors exhibit higher levels of anxiety and stress-related disorders, suggesting that the trauma experienced by their ancestors has a lasting impact on their genetic makeup (Rodriguez, 2015).

The more we recognize the impact ancestral experiences have on our emotional and stress responses, the more pressing the need to address generational traumas becomes. It can change inherited emotional patterns, improve our emotional default state, and promote better mental health and well-being for ourselves and future generations.

The stronger your emotional resilience, the higher your emotional baseline will become. Emotional resilience is the ability to navigate both internal and external challenges without being overwhelmed by emotional turmoil. Building this resilience is one of the most effective ways to elevate your emotional baseline and create a more stable, positive state of mind.

Before creating meaningful change, you must first acknowledge and understand what needs to be transformed. Shifting an inherited emotional baseline takes a mix of self-awareness, healing work, and intentional lifestyle changes. By addressing generational trauma, we open the door to deeper emotional well-being and lasting transformation. Here are some strategies to help you get started:

Understand Your Roots

Explore your family history to uncover any traumas or significant challenges your ancestors may have faced. Recognizing these patterns can provide valuable insights into your own emotional landscape. Take the time to research concepts like emotional DNA and generational trauma. Reading books or articles on epigenetics and the impact of inherited trauma can help you gain insight into your own emotional tendencies. The more you understand, the better prepared you'll be to break the cycle and create a healthier emotional legacy.

Explore Plant Medicine

Plant medicines like ayahuasca, psilocybin, tepezcohuite, and ibogaine are gaining attention for their powerful role in trauma healing. These natural substances can create deeply transformative experiences in controlled, therapeutic settings, allowing individuals to face and process unresolved, deep-rooted traumas. Many people find that these experiences bring new clarity to inherited emotional patterns, offering deep emotional release and healing that traditional methods sometimes take years to reach.

It's crucial to pursue these treatments under professional guidance; doing so will ensure both safety and effectiveness. The field of psychedelic-assisted therapy is rapidly evolving, with early research showing promising results for treating trauma, depression, and anxiety. This holistic approach can provide a powerful set of tools to address and heal generational trauma. I'll dive deeper into this topic later in Chapter 12.

Expand Your Support Network

Joining support groups creates a sense of community and shared understanding, reminding you that you're not alone in your journey. Taking part in cultural or ancestral rituals and practices can also be deeply healing, helping you connect with your roots and find a stronger sense of identity and belonging.

Genetic Counseling

Another option to consider is genetic counseling. Genetic counseling is a process where trained professionals help individuals understand how their genes may affect their health, inheritance risks, and medical or reproductive options. It can provide insights and personalized strategies for managing inherited emotional baselines.

Practical Steps to Healing Generational Trauma

1. Do some digging into the past but be considerate in how you approach the matter. While your quest can bring healing in other family members, too, be aware that they're likely not in the same place as you're in the process of healing and growth. Your quest may cause unwanted emotions to surface and you're likely to stumble into resistance if they're not ready to open up. While it can be

frustrating, remember there's usually more than one way to learn what you need to know to set yourself free.

2. Cognitive restructuring can help reprogram your emotional baseline by changing your perspective on past experiences and events. It allows you to view things from a more positive viewpoint. Cognitive reframing is a mental exercise that changes how we see and interpret a situation or event.

    a. When faced with a challenging situation, write down your initial thoughts and feelings.

    b. Ask yourself if there's another way to view the situation. What positive aspects can you find?

    c. Reframe your thoughts to focus on growth and learning opportunities.

3. For change to last, it must become part of your new identity. If you've always seen yourself as someone with a poor emotional baseline, start by shifting that narrative. Envision yourself as someone who naturally experiences joy, embraces pleasure, and optimizes life.

    a. Visualize your ideal self. See yourself as someone who possesses a strong emotional foundation. What are these individual's habits, beliefs, and behaviors?

    b. Incorporate these habits into your daily routine.

    c. Affirm your new identity regularly: "I find joy in everyday moments."

How Social Circles Affect Emotional Well-being

Positive, supportive relationships can lift your mood, reduce stress, and foster resilience. Toxic relationships, on the other hand, can contribute to anxiety, depression, and emotional instability.

In 1938, Harvard University launched the Grant Study to determine the reason for longevity and vitality. The study followed the lives of over 700 men, including the then-young John F. Kennedy, keeping track of their life events and perceptions of experiences during the good and bad times (Waldinger & Schulz, 2023).

This research has shown that having a supportive social network can help buffer the effects of stress. Access to a social support system helps regulate emotional responses, promoting a more stable emotional baseline, even during adversity.

It found that lasting, meaningful relationships are the key to longevity and happiness. People are social beings, and we need this connection to thrive. Strong, happy, and healthy social connections contribute to our overall emotional health.

Exposure to chronic stress, such as that stemming from negative social interactions, leads to elevated levels of cortisol, the body's primary stress hormone. This increase in cortisol can impair emotional regulation and is associated with an increased risk of developing anxiety, depression, and other mood disorders.

Think of the last time you walked into a room after an argument was over. Could you sense negativity in the air without anyone saying a word? Emotions are vibrations and contain energy. Negative and positive feelings (like all other emotions) are energy waves which affect the mood of everyone in the vicinity. This phenomenon is known as emotional contagion. A study found that emotions can spread through social networks like a virus (Chu et al., 2024). For instance, happiness was shown to spread up to three degrees of separation, meaning your happiness can affect not only your friends but also their friends and their friends. Sadly, negative vibes have a much further reach.

Getting Practical in Surrounding Yourself with Positive People

Grab your journal for the next exercise.

1. Write down the names of people who positively affect your life and describe how they make you feel.

2. Note individuals who bring stress or negativity and reflect on how they affect your emotions.

3. Create a plan to spend more time with positive influences and set boundaries with negative ones.

4. Identify specific steps you can take to build supportive relationships while minimizing your exposure to toxic ones.

By surrounding yourself with positive, supportive people, you can significantly enhance your emotional baseline, leading to a more balanced, resilient, and fulfilling life. Similarly, surrounding yourself with the wrong support network can keep your armor intact.

Remember that even if your emotional default has largely been shaped by generational trauma, it doesn't have to be your permanent state. **You have the power to change it.**

Emotional Intelligence (EQ)

While it may be possible to separate emotional intelligence (EQ) from your emotional default, it's not ideal, as the two are interconnected. Each profoundly influences the other, making it difficult to address one without considering the impact on the other.

Emotional intelligence is your brain's hidden power. Imagine your brain as a highly skilled orchestra, each instrument representing a different emotion. When your emotions work in harmony, your brain produces a beautiful symphony, enabling you to navigate the complexities of life with grace. EQ is about mastering that orchestra.

Through the remarkable power of neuroplasticity (mentioned in Chapter 1), you can train yourself to manage your emotions with skill and precision.

Mastering Your Feelings

Emotional intelligence is the ability to recognize, understand, and manage your own emotions while also navigating and responding to the emotions of others in a healthy and effective way. Remember the last time you felt overwhelmed—perhaps it was anger, frustration, or sadness at play. It was likely your amygdala, the brain's emotional epicenter, running the show. When the amygdala takes over, emotions can feel chaotic and all-consuming. But here's the good news: it doesn't have to stay that way.

With practice, you can strengthen your prefrontal cortex, the brain's hub for rational thinking and emotional regulation. This empowers you to take back control, enabling emotional intelligence to drive your actions instead of being ruled by impulsive reactions.

Cognitive Reappraisal

Cognitive reappraisal shifts how you see things, especially in emotionally intense situations. It's a way of taking control of your perspective instead of letting your emotions run the show. Similar to adjusting the focus on a camera, you bring what's important into clarity while letting the unnecessary noise fade into the background.

Imagine being stuck in traffic when someone suddenly cuts you off. Your first reaction might be frustration or anger, but then you pause and ask yourself, "What's another way to look at this?" Perhaps that driver is rushing to an emergency, or they made a simple mistake—just like you might have on a stressful day. By reframing the situation, you reduce the emotional intensity, allowing yourself to respond with calm and control rather than reacting impulsively.

Increased Self-Awareness and Self-Regulation

Self-awareness is at the core of emotional intelligence. Without it, you're like a ship sailing without a compass, reacting to the world without understanding the reasons behind your emotions. Self-awareness is the ability to step outside yourself and observe your emotional responses objectively.

For instance, if you feel anxious before a presentation, self-awareness allows you to pinpoint the root cause—perhaps you fear being judged. Recognizing this pattern is the first step to self-awareness. From there, you can work on desensitizing yourself to that fear by practicing in front of a supportive audience or reframing your mindset about public speaking, seeing it as an opportunity to connect rather than a performance to be judged. Over time, this self-awareness fosters emotional resilience, enabling you to approach similar situations with confidence.

After self-awareness comes self-regulation, which is the ability to manage your emotions rather than letting them take the lead. It's about responding thoughtfully instead of reacting impulsively. Think of it as being a thermostat instead of a thermometer. A thermometer simply reacts to the temperature, while a thermostat actively adjusts and maintains balance no matter what's happening in the environment.

One technique I often recommend is the 5-5-5 breathing method: Inhale for five seconds, hold for five seconds, and exhale for five seconds. This simple breathing exercise signals to your nervous system that it's time to relax, helping you regain control during emotionally intense moments.

Deliberate practice can strengthen your prefrontal cortex, the part of the brain responsible for rational thinking and emotional regulation. This practice helps you regain control, allowing emotional intelligence to guide your actions rather than react impulsively.

The way you talk about your emotions shapes how you experience them. By changing your inner dialogue, you improve your emotional intelligence. For example, instead of saying, "I am anxious," try saying, "I am feeling anxious." This subtle shift reminds you that emotions are temporary states, not defining characteristics of who you are.

Empathy

Empathy is the bridge that connects us. It's not about feeling for someone; it's about understanding and sharing someone else's feelings. By showing empathy, you create a real emotional connection that makes the other person feel seen, heard, and understood on a deeper level.

Empathy engages the same neural circuits in the brain that are activated when we experience emotions. This "mirroring" effect builds trust, strengthens relationships, and encourages cooperation. Empathy lays the foundation for genuine connection and understanding, whether you're leading a team, resolving a conflict, or comforting a friend.

To build empathy, practice active listening. When someone speaks to you, focus fully on their words without planning your next response. When you acknowledge someone's feelings with a statement like, "I can see how frustrating that must be," you open the door for empathy to grow and create a space where connection feels natural and safe.

Random acts of kindness are another powerful way to boost emotional intelligence by fostering empathy and creating positive feedback loops in the brain. When you perform acts of kindness, your brain releases oxytocin, the "love hormone," which enhances mood and strengthens social bonds. By committing to small acts of kindness each day, you not only improve the lives of others but also elevate your own emotional well-being.

Exposure Therapy

Just as exposure therapy helps people overcome phobias, it's also a powerful tool for reconditioning emotional responses. By gradually facing emotionally challenging situations and applying emotional intelligence techniques, you train your brain to respond with calm and control instead of fear or overwhelm. Over time, this positive exposure re-trains your emotional responses, helping you navigate tough moments with confidence and ease.

This technique is great for anyone who struggles with criticism or confrontation. By seeking out constructive feedback in a safe and supportive environment, you can build emotional resilience, improve your communication skills, and reframe feedback as an opportunity for growth rather than a personal attack. This technique is great for anyone who struggles with criticism or confrontation. By seeking constructive feedback in a safe and supportive environment, you can build emotional resilience, improve your communication skills, and reframe feedback as an opportunity for growth rather than a personal attack.

Getting Practical in Rewiring for Emotional Mastery

1. Pay attention to your emotions. When you feel a wave of emotion rising, challenge yourself to shift your perspective and ask, "How can I see this differently?" Notice how your feelings change when you do this. It might feel hard at first, but once you've done it, you'll realize it wasn't as difficult as it seemed. It's just like building any new habit—repeat it enough, and it'll eventually become your new normal.

2. Once you know your current state, it's easier to identify what you want and don't want in your life. Whenever you change anything, identify what you want to replace it with. This technique helps you gain clarity on what you aim to achieve through emotional mastery.

3. Practice active listening daily. Choose at least one conversation where you give the speaker your full, undivided attention, no distractions, just genuine focus. Pay attention to how this shifts their response and deepens the connection. Active listening isn't just a skill; it's also a powerful act of kindness.

By practicing self-awareness, self-regulation, empathy, and positive social interactions, you can rewire your brain for emotional mastery. Building emotional intelligence creates trust within yourself and others, paving the way for lasting success and fulfillment.

Chapter 8:
Finding Strength Beyond the Visible

Without the spiritual component, the artist works with a crucial disadvantage. The spiritual world provides a sense of wonder and a degree of open-mindedness not always found within the confines of science. The world of reason can be narrow and filled with dead ends, while a spiritual viewpoint is limitless and invites fantastic possibilities. The unseen world is boundless. —Rick Rubin

In a world fractured by different belief systems and religions, explaining spirituality is no easy task. Many who identify as spiritual see religion as too rigid, confining the boundless nature of spirit. At the same time, the religious often criticize the spiritual for being too inclusive and refusing to commit to a singular path or doctrine. It's a constant push and pull—one side finds freedom, whereas the other seeks structure, making it hard to find common ground.

At this stage, labeling yourself isn't the priority. What matters is awakening the spirit within you. Through this connection, you tap into the boundless potential to live a richer and more meaningful life. Spirituality offers a doorway to answering many philosophical questions. It empowers you to explore questions about life's meaning and pursue your purpose. It's also a way to cope more effectively with stress, anxiety, and depression.

Many of us still struggle to acknowledge and embrace the spirit within. I believed the world was only as real as what I could see, touch, or control. If I couldn't measure it, I couldn't trust it. Life has a way of revealing its deeper truths. It shows us that the most powerful forces are often the ones we can't see. It teaches us that the very things we think we don't have time or energy for are the ones that make life meaningful. The more I leaned into what I couldn't see, the quiet knowing, the trust in something greater, the energy that moves through all things—the more I realized that this is where real freedom lives.

When I first began my journey inward, I had no idea I was stepping into the spirit realm. I was just trying to heal and lighten the weight of my emotional baggage. But as I softened and let my walls come down, I sensed something greater—a subtle yet undeniable presence. It was a quiet knowing, a gentle, guiding force rising from deep within me. This marked the start of a new relationship—not just with me, but with something far greater. I realized there was a force within me and all around me that I could lean on for strength, clarity, and peace. What started as a quest for healing became a journey to understand my purpose.

It was only once I connected with my spirit that healing could occur.

Learning to Listen

Connecting to spirit is about quieting yourself enough to listen. Our lives are filled with noise—distractions, doubts, and fears that keep us from hearing our inner voice. Spirit speaks softly; it doesn't shout over the chaos. In those quiet moments, pauses between breaths, I sensed something steady and wise. At first, it felt strange, as though I was just imagining things. But the more I practiced being still, the more I could recognize the voice of spirit guiding me.

Sometimes, it's a gentle nudge, an urge to pause before reacting. Other times, a sense of comfort appears out of nowhere, reminding me that I'm connected to a much larger force. When fear creeps in—the fear of being vulnerable, of showing softness in a world that rewards toughness—I feel that inner presence reassuring me. It reminds me that my strength comes from my alignment with the spirit within.

Letting Go to Receive

You can't receive anything with a clenched fist. To welcome something new, you must first let go and make space for it. The same applies to connecting with spirit—it requires surrender, trust, and an open heart.

Connecting to spirit meant unlearning the idea that I had to do it all on my own. For so long, I believed that strength was about control, about holding it all together. But spirit asks us to let go, to surrender. This means allowing us to be supported by something far greater than ourselves. It means realizing we don't have to carry every burden by ourselves and don't have to walk this journey alone.

Trusting in something I couldn't see, or control didn't come naturally. But the more I released my grip on the need to manage every detail, the more I discovered a calm, grounding force within me. It was as if the universe was whispering, *"You don't have to do this alone."* With every act of surrender, I felt stronger, more connected, and better equipped to face whatever life brought my way.

Inviting Spirit into Daily Life

This connection isn't something I save for quiet moments or meditation; it's a daily practice. I've learned to invite spirit into everything, from the smallest decisions to the biggest challenges. Before a tough conversation or a big decision, I take a moment to pause, breathe, and ask for guidance. This simple act shifts my energy and helps me approach situations with clarity instead of fear.

Sometimes, connecting to spirit is as simple as noticing the beauty around me. I observe how the sun's rays shine through trees, the sound of laughter, or just the feeling of gratitude for being alive and healthy. These moments remind me that I'm part of something much larger than myself. They ground me in a sense of purpose and connection that transcends my day-to-day worries.

Trusting the Signs

One of the most transformative aspects of connecting with spirit has been learning to trust the signs. Spirit subtly communicates through synchronicities, gut feelings, and signs that appear when you need them most. At first, I dismissed these as coincidences, but over time I've seen them as the spirit's way of guiding me.

There's comfort in knowing that I'm not walking this path on my own. When I'm uncertain or feeling lost, I ask for a sign. Sometimes, it comes as a song lyric, repeating numbers, or a conversation that answers a question I've been struggling with. Spirit speaks personally and profoundly, reminding me that I'm supported and loved, even when I can't see the bigger picture. It never screams, shouts, or forces itself. It's gentle, always, and therefore demands a quiet heart and mind to be heard.

Connecting to spirit has given me a newfound strength.

This connection to spirit isn't about escaping reality but facing it with greater peace and purpose. It's about knowing that my fears or past don't define me. This deeper connection reminds me of who I am. Spirit gives me the courage to live fully, love deeply, and show up in the world as my authentic self.

There was a time when this felt impossible for me—at least without a drink in hand. I relied on alcohol to lower my defenses, to quiet the walls I had built around myself. As the saying goes, *"A drunk man's words are a sober man's thoughts."* And for me, that couldn't have been truer. Only when I drank could I let my guard down, allowing the softer, more loving parts of me to surface— the parts I was too afraid to show the world when I was sober. The moment the drinks wore off, my true self vanished once more, retreating behind the fortress of armor I had built to protect me. It took a lot of time and hard work to peel through all the layers, but once I did, I could let go of the anger and darkness and be myself without the need for a drink. I was able to naturally exude the love and kindness within me. Sometimes, a mere chip in your armor will help you realize you don't need outside substances to be yourself.

Only when you step beyond the confines of your armor do you realize that the person you thought you were wasn't really you— it was just a reflection of your defenses. My armor projected anger and aggression, and for a long time, I mistook that for my identity. It wasn't until I broke free from that hardened exterior that I discovered my true self. Now, I stand fully in who I am, unguarded and at peace. And the best part? I genuinely love this version of me, and I love sharing her with the world.

Spirituality as an Antidepressant

According to the studies of Dr. Lisa Miller, author of The Awakened Brain, the brain areas reacting to spiritual experiences are the same areas that light up with the use of SSRIs widely prescribed to treat depression. Do I recommend getting off your meds while taking a deep dive in exploring your spiritual side? No! But it's important to recognize that scientific research is actively exploring how these findings can serve as a foundation for incorporating spirituality as a complementary approach to mental health treatment (A New Study Led by TC's Lisa Miller Pinpoints Where and How the Brain Registers Spiritual Experience, 2018).

Embracing the Spirit

The voice of spirit becomes clear when you quiet your mind, heart, and surroundings, creating space to truly listen. For some, this quiet time takes the form of prayer; for others, it's meditation, mindful practices, or time spent in nature. While all these methods are powerful, the key is consistency. Like any relationship, your connection with spirit requires time, effort, and intention to deepen and grow. As your bond strengthens, consulting with spirit throughout your day becomes more natural and effortless, offering guidance and clarity when needed.

Seek the Good in Others

If forgiveness is the first step and acceptance is the second, then seeking the good is undoubtedly the third. Once you learn to accept people for who they are and not let their actions affect you, it's easier to recognize the good in them. Every one of us carries light and shadow aspects to our personality, so what you see in others often depends on where you focus your attention. The more accepting you become, the more you'll see the goodness in others and connect with their spirit.

Getting Practical in Embracing Your Spirit

Spiritual growth blossoms through consistent reflection and practice. Think of your connection with spirit like any other relationship in your life. At first, it might feel unfamiliar, even a little awkward. But the more time you invest in it, the more natural it becomes, and over time, that bond deepens and strengthens.

Set aside time each day for spiritual reflection. You can explore different practices to nurture your connection with spirit during this time. I've listed a few options below. While adding variety to your routine is beneficial, you might also find that certain practices resonate more deeply with you. These can become your go-to rituals, grounding and enriching your spiritual journey.

- Take a moment to notice the natural world around you. Can you see the treetops from your window or a garden in the distance? Is there a park nearby where you can escape for a while? Maybe you're lucky enough to live close to nature and can immerse yourself in it often. Wherever you are, let these glimpses of the earth's beauty ground you, offering a sense of peace and quiet inspiration.

- Take this time to reflect on your connection to all living beings—and, ultimately, to the universe itself. Consider what this connection means, especially in moments of sadness or loneliness. What if, instead of feeling separate or unworthy, you recognized that you are an essential part of something vast and infinite? The universe cannot reject you because you inherently belong. Embracing this truth might just soften the edges of your self-protection, making it easier to let go of the emotional armor you no longer need.

- Connecting with spirit means taking the moral high ground. It's rarely easy—in fact, it's often the hardest choice—but it becomes more manageable when you remember that you're deeply connected to everyone and everything, with spiritual guidance always there to support you. Though the journey may be difficult, the clarity and peace you find makes everything worth it.

Chapter 9:
Release Your Subconscious Power

Reality is created by the mind; we can change our reality by changing our mind.–Plato

Rhonda Byrne's publication of *The Secret* reignited a global fascination with manifestation. I say "reignited" because there's nothing new about the concept—it's been around and successfully employed for ages by those who understand the nature of manifestation and how to use it effectively. This is something Eckart Tolle reminds us of when he says,

> "The secret of manifestation is expressed in one simple statement by Jesus, and that encapsulates all the books that have been written on manifestation and will ever be written on manifestation…one simple sentence, he (Jesus) says, 'When you pray for something, believe that it has been given or that you already have it then you'll receive it.'"

Tolle explains that the key to manifestation lies not in believing you *will receive* what you desire someday but in embodying the mindset that *it's already yours.* But how does that work? How do you convince yourself you already have something?

As overwhelming as it might be, when you explore the incredible power of the subconscious mind and learn how to work with it, you realize it's not as hard as it seems. The life you dream of is closer than you think and making it a reality involves committing to harnessing the power within you.

Our beliefs powerfully affect our reality, and at the heart of it all lies the subconscious mind. Operating mostly beneath our awareness, this hidden part of us holds immense influence over our thoughts, feelings, and behaviors. It's where our deepest beliefs, memories, and unconscious patterns live, subtly steering the course of our lives.

When we start to understand and harness the incredible power of the subconscious, we can experience profound transformation and step into the full potential of the life we've always dreamed of.

This is an understanding presented in the teachings of many renowned spiritual and mindset experts.

Neville Goddard's teachings emphasize the profound influence of the subconscious mind in shaping our reality. He famously stated, "Assume the feeling of your wish fulfilled and observe the route that your attention follows." According to Goddard, we can manifest our deepest desires by impressing them onto the subconscious mind through the power of imagination.

Joseph Murphy, the author of *The Power of Your Subconscious Mind*, echoed this sentiment in his exploration of the transformative power of subconscious programming. He wrote, "The subconscious mind is ruled by suggestion. It accepts all suggestions; it does not argue with you—it fulfills your wishes." Murphy was a strong advocate for using positive affirmations and visualization as tools to influence the subconscious, enabling us to create meaningful change and manifest the life we desire.

Carl Jung pioneered raising awareness of the profound importance of the subconscious mind. Jung stressed that understanding and working with the subconscious is essential for achieving psychological wholeness and deeper self-awareness. He encouraged us to take control of our subconscious to reclaim power over our conscious lives. As he famously stated, "Until you make the unconscious conscious, it will direct your life, and you will call it fate."

By the time you hit 35, nearly everything about you—your behaviors, emotional reactions, habits, beliefs, and attitudes—runs on autopilot. It's like an operating system that's been programmed through years of repetition. Only about 5% of your thoughts and actions come from a conscious, intentional place. The rest? It's muscle memory—subconscious patterns playing on a loop, shaping how you see yourself and the world around you.

And here's the challenge: if that 95% is filled with outdated stories, limiting beliefs, or deeply ingrained fears, your conscious mind—your dreams, your goals, your best intentions—is fighting an uphill battle. It's like trying to steer a ship when the autopilot is locked in the opposite direction. If you want to change your life, you must go deeper than surface-level motivation. You must reprogram the subconscious patterns running the show.

More recently, best-selling author Robin Sharma echoed this idea with his powerful statement: *"Everything is created twice, first in the mind and then in reality."*

Scientific Proof of the Power of the Subconscious Mind

A study published in the *Journal of Neuroscience* revealed that placebos can trigger the brain's endorphin system, reducing pain similarly to actual medication.

The mind is so powerful that what we believe to be true can shape our reality. So, when patients believe they're receiving treatment, even if it's just a sugar pill, their condition often improves. This demonstrates how the subconscious mind can affect physical health through belief alone.

Unlocking the Subconscious Through Heart-Brain Coherence

Dr. Joe Dispenza has spent years studying the connection between the mind and body, particularly the concept of heart-brain coherence—a state where the heart and brain are in sync, leading to greater emotional balance, mental clarity, and overall well-being. He teaches that by intentionally cultivating elevated emotions such as gratitude, love, and joy, we can shift our internal state, influence our autonomic nervous system, and create real, measurable changes in our bodies and lives.

His work aligns with decades of research conducted by the HeartMath Institute, a leading organization in studying the heart's intelligence and its impact on human health and performance. Their research shows that the heart has its own nervous system, which constantly communicates with the brain, affecting cognitive function, emotions, and physiological responses. When we generate coherence—a state where our heart's rhythm is smooth and stable—the brain and body function optimally, reducing stress and enhancing mental clarity.

The HeartMath Institute has developed practical techniques to help individuals achieve this state. One of their core practices, the Quick Coherence Technique, involves three simple steps: directing attention to the heart, slowing the breath, and consciously activating a positive emotion. Studies have shown that practicing this technique regularly can help reduce anxiety, improve decision-making, and create a greater sense of ease and emotional resilience.

The idea behind both Dispenza's teachings and HeartMath's research is simple: when we shift from survival-based emotions like fear and stress to elevated emotions like love and gratitude, we create a different physiological and neurological environment within ourselves. This shift isn't just theoretical, it's measurable! Research has shown that when people enter a coherent state, their heart rhythms become more ordered, cortisol levels decrease, and brain function improves.

By learning to regulate our emotions and achieve heart-brain coherence, we tap into a deeper level of subconscious power. This practice allows us to break free from old, limiting patterns and create a new reality—one where we're not just reacting to life but consciously shaping it. The ability to align our thoughts and emotions with our desired future is one of the most powerful tools we have, and it all starts with learning to regulate what's happening inside of us first.

Getting Practical in Developing Awareness of Thoughts and Emotions

Commit to the following practice for seven continuous days to explore its impact on your life. To stay on track with your transformation's progress, why not record your thoughts, feelings, and behaviors?

Early Morning

Take some quiet time to do this exercise shortly after you wake up. Divide your journal pages into two columns: on one side, list the thoughts and feelings you don't like, and on the other, write down the ones you do like.

Each morning, take a few moments to reflect on the thoughts and emotions that arise. Write down the ones that feel right and those that don't. For the ones that don't, reframe them into something that aligns with how you want to feel. This practice helps you develop greater self-awareness and shifts your mindset toward one that empowers and supports you.

Throughout the Day

Maintain a consistent record of your thoughts and emotions throughout the day. Use the same two-column approach. When you experience a noteworthy thought or emotion, write it down in the corresponding column.

Consider the impact of these thoughts and emotions on your overall life and actions.

Evening Routine

Repeat the morning exercise just before bedtime to conclude your day.

- Review your daily entries with a keen eye for recurring patterns. Notice how certain positive or negative themes reappear and reflect on their impact.

- Consider which thoughts—uplifting or discouraging—impact your behavior and overall mindset throughout the day.

A Few More Points to Consider

Joy multiplies when we shift our focus from scarcity to abundance. Consciously appreciating your current circumstances can deepen your self-awareness and sense of contentment. This doesn't mean ignoring areas where you need improvement. It's about finding the balance between striving for more and being thankful for where you currently are.

Worrying about the future creates stress, and dwelling on the past usually leads to regret. Genuine joy comes from being present. When you focus on the here and now, you can fully engage in the moment, making it both meaningful and productive.

Shift Your Focus to Cultivate Greater Happiness

You can shift your mood and even improve your biochemistry by focusing on the present moment, what you have, and what's within your control. Focusing on what you can control shifts your mindset from feeling helpless to acting and making progress. On the other hand, fixating on things outside your control only leads to frustration and a sense of powerlessness. By channeling your energy into what you can influence, you can create a sense of progress and mastery over your life.

The present moment is free from fear, worry, or regret. Just imagine how different you'd feel if all that mattered was this moment. No stressing over bills—they're not due until the end of the month, no need to regret past actions—they've already happened. The past is behind us, the future isn't promised, so the present is all we have. It's called the present for a reason—it's a gift and the only time that exists.

Seeing Is Not Believing

There's a common saying that seeing is believing. However, it's the other way around...believing is seeing. Your mind perceives what it believes to be true, and once a belief is formed, your brain finds ways to validate it. So, it's so important to cultivate positive beliefs about yourself and your life. The mind is wired to confirm what it accepts as truth; your brain will work to make that belief a reality.

Belief Audit Exercise

1. Clearly articulate your intentions to activate the power of your subconscious mind

2. Visualize your goals as already fulfilled and fully embrace the emotions of achieving them.

3. Identify a belief holding you back.

4. Identify and document evidence that contradicts this belief.

5. Replace the limiting belief with a positive affirmation.

6. Act "as if" your desired outcomes aren't just future possibilities, but already your current reality.

This practice builds your confidence and motivation, turning challenges into steppingstones that push you closer to your vision with purpose and clarity. When you combine intention, belief, and action, your subconscious becomes a powerful ally in helping you achieve your goals.

Achievement Without Satisfaction

The biggest failure is success without fulfillment. Reaching your goals without feeling any real satisfaction makes those achievements feel empty. Fulfillment is more than just hitting milestones—it's about enjoying the process, finding purpose, and creating meaning along the way. True fulfillment comes from growing as a person, making an impact, and giving back to others in a rewarding way.

Real success happens when your achievements align with your values and make a meaningful contribution. You feel connected to the positive difference you're making in the world or in the lives of others. This harmony between external accomplishments and inner fulfillment transforms success into something deeply rewarding.

Fulfillment isn't a destination—it's woven into the process of growth, contribution, and knowing you're making a positive impact. Even the biggest accomplishments can feel empty without that sense of purpose. When you infuse your goals with purpose and find joy in both the journey and the difference you make along the way, you turn success into something meaningful and lasting.

Reprogramming your subconscious mind involves cultivating empowering attitudes, focusing on what matters to you, and rewriting your internal narrative. Adopting a more positive outlook and consciously redirecting your focus can create a more joyful and fulfilling life where your beliefs shape your reality. Always remember you have the power to define how you perceive the world. Embrace that power and watch as it transforms your entire being.

The methods we've discussed for tapping into your mind's potential are simple, but we've just scratched the surface. We must explore even more advanced techniques, such as neuro-linguistic programming, to understand what's possible.

Neuro-Linguistic Programming

Neuro-linguistic programming (NLP) is a psychological approach designed to identify and reshape cognitive patterns, behaviors, and language to achieve specific goals and enhance mental and emotional well-being. Developed in the 1970s by Richard Bandler and John Grinder, NLP has since gained widespread recognition for its effectiveness in personal development, as a therapy, and in improving interpersonal communication (Shekerinov, 2023).

NLP emphasizes the powerful role of language in shaping our thoughts and perceptions. Since our understanding of reality is heavily influenced by the language we use, NLP operates on the idea that we can alter our perception of reality by changing our language patterns.

Anchoring is an NLP technique that connects a specific physical or emotional state to a certain trigger, allowing you to access that feeling whenever you like. It's like training your brain to feel a certain way when something specific happens. Think about how your favorite song makes you feel happy or excited every time you hear it—that's anchoring in action! It's the same idea as Pavlov's experiment, where he taught his dogs to associate the sound of a bell with being fed. With anchoring, you're essentially conditioning yourself to feel calm, happy, or confident whenever needed.

Steps to Master Anchoring

1. To create an anchor, select the emotional state you wish to access, such as confidence, calmness, or motivation.

2. Think of a peak experience when you naturally felt this desired state. Close your eyes and fully immerse yourself in the memory, recalling the sights, sounds, and feelings.

3. Choose an anchor by selecting a physical gesture or touch (such as pressing your thumb and forefinger together) to serve as your anchor.

4. As you reach the peak of the emotional state in your memory, perform the chosen gesture. Repeat this several times to strengthen the association.

5. In future situations where you need to access the desired state, use the anchor gesture to trigger the desired emotion.

Our Perception Shapes Our Reality

The way we see the world isn't how it is; it's how we perceive it to be. Our perspective on life, the world, and everything in it is shaped by our background, our values, and the language we use to express ourselves. What we see is our interpretation of reality. That's why if you don't like what you're seeing, feeling, or experiencing, you can shift how you perceive it. What feels real to you might look completely different to someone else, because their perspective is shaped by a different set of experiences and beliefs.

Getting Practical with Reframing

1. Choose a situation or behavior you want to reframe, particularly one that tends to bring up negative emotions or thoughts.

2. Explore different interpretations of the situation. Ask yourself questions like, "What else could this mean?" or "How can I view this in a more positive way?"

3. Adopt the new perspective and notice how it shifts your feelings. Keep practicing seeing the situation through this more positive lens until it becomes your go-to approach.

Rapport Building

Building rapport is a key NLP technique for improving communication and building positive relationships. By subtly mirroring and matching the verbal and non-verbal cues of others, you establish a deeper sense of connection and trust.

How to Build Rapport

1. Pay close attention to the body language, tone of voice, and language patterns of the person you're communicating with.

2. Subtly mirror or match their posture, gestures, and tone of voice. Use similar language or phrases to create a sense of familiarity.

3. Once you've built rapport, you can adjust your behavior to steer the interaction in a positive direction. If the connection is solid, the other person will usually follow your lead.

Chapter 10:
Fix Relationships with Imago
Therapy

When we were babies, we didn't smile sweetly at our mothers to get them to take care of us. We didn't pinpoint our discomfort by putting it into words. We simply opened our mouths and screamed. And it didn't take us long to learn that the louder we screamed, the quicker they came. The success of this tactic was turned into an "imprint," a part of our stored memory about how to get the world to respond to our needs: When you are frustrated, provoke the people around you. –Harville Hendrix

If you had the choice, would you pick a different upbringing? Different parents? A different neighborhood to grow up in?

For the longest time, I thought my answer would be a resounding *yes*! But if not for my upbringing and every experience that shaped me along the way, I wouldn't be the person I am today. I wouldn't be sitting here, writing this book, and connecting with you. What a privilege that would be to miss out on.

The highs and lows we face are all part of the human experience. Each moment offers a lesson, but the truth is, those lessons don't always resonate the first time. We often repeat the same mistakes repeatedly before wisdom finally sets in.

One such lesson was repeatedly going into relationships that replicated the relationship I witnessed between my parents. For years, I carried deep resentment toward my father for his infidelity, but the truth was, my feelings toward my mother weren't much lighter. I couldn't understand why she stayed.

Why do we find ourselves in relationships—romantic or otherwise—that carry the same weight we once longed to escape in childhood? Often, these patterns slip by unnoticed because it's always easier to analyze others than to examine ourselves. It's simple to question the woman who grew up watching her father drink, only to marry an alcoholic, or the one who swore never to tolerate infidelity, yet somehow ends up with a cheater. The cycle isn't always obvious until we're deep in it, repeating what once felt familiar, even if it was painful.

The answer to these pressing questions can be found in Imago therapy.

The saying "No man is an island" perfectly captures human nature—we're wired for connection. Our relationships shape our lives in profound ways, yet maintaining healthy, lasting bonds isn't always easy. It takes intention, effort, and the right tools to nurture connections that support and sustain us.

Imago therapy, created by Dr. Harville Hendrix and Dr. Helen LaKelly Hunt, is a helpful and effective method for understanding and resolving interpersonal issues. While its primary focus is romantic bonds, it can work as effectively in family relationships. It answers the question, "Why do couples fight?". Still, it covers a much wider area of concern and deserves an in-depth exploration of its fundamental ideas, advantages, and practical measures for using its approaches in daily life.

The Basis of Imago Therapy

Imago therapy is rooted in the idea that we're subconsciously drawn to partners who reflect both the positive and negative traits of our primary caregivers—whether they were our parents, guardians, or grandparents.

This attraction stems from a deep-seated desire to confront and heal unresolved childhood wounds. The term "imago" refers to the internalized image of our caregivers, shaped during childhood, which profoundly influences how we navigate relationships and choose our partners.

This solution is built upon the following key pillars:

- This kind of attraction happens on a subconscious level. Without realizing it, we're naturally drawn to partners who carry both the good and bad traits of our primary caregivers. Often, we're too caught up in trying to heal those unresolved childhood wounds—or too close to the pain they've created—to see it clearly. This distorted lens keeps us from recognizing how much we use our adult relationships to work through what we didn't heal as children.

- Imago therapy suggests that romantic relationships provide a unique opportunity for healing through connection. When partners take the time to understand and acknowledge each other's childhood wounds, they create space for growth and healing. Identifying unmet needs within family dynamics and recognizing recurring patterns or cycles can further support this process.

- Imago therapy focuses on the importance of intentional dialogue. It's about communicating clearly and is paired with active listening. This kind of deliberate approach helps create understanding, deepens empathy, and strengthens the connection between partners.

Imago therapy is known as a powerful way to heal childhood wounds, but it requires both partners to be fully committed—not just to their own growth but to the growth of their relationship. That means recognizing subconscious patterns, addressing them head-on, and working together to build a conscious and fulfilling connection.

The Advantages of Imago Therapy

At its core, Imago therapy is about healing not just our relationships, but ourselves, too. It can shift toxic dynamics into spaces that feel safe and supportive, allowing us to be more vulnerable and authentic in the connections that matter most.

- Imago therapy helps partners get to the root of their conflicts, guiding them to recognize and understand their emotional triggers. This awareness fosters more empathy and strengthens bonds.

- Using purposeful dialogue helps improve communication. It allows partners to express themselves openly and listen empathetically. It creates an environment of greater acceptance where unconditional love can be showcased, making it easier to be authentic.

- By acknowledging and addressing unresolved childhood wounds, partners can break free from harmful patterns and begin healing.

- Imago therapy creates a healthy, supportive, and nurturing environment, paving the way for a stronger, longer-lasting partnership.

Balanced Conversation

This process consists of three primary stages: mirroring, validating, and empathizing, but I want to expand on mirroring.

Mirroring is when the listener repeats back the speaker's words to ensure they've understood correctly, and nothing gets lost in translation.

It also helps the speaker feel heard, acknowledged, and valued.

So, how does this play out in real life?

Mirroring will often begin with a phrase:

"Based on my understanding of your words..."

This lets the speaker know that their feelings, thoughts, and perspectives matter. It lets them know their point of view is being heard and acknowledged, even if disagreements exist. It's a way of showing respect for their emotions and experiences.

Another example is, "I may not fully understand, but I'm willing to listen and try…"

It's a statement of empathy, showing the listener genuinely cares about and respects the speaker's emotions.

Alternatively, you can say, "I can see this stirs certain emotions within you…"

But there's another side to mirroring that's nonverbal—and it can be even more impactful since words are only a small part of communication.

Subtly reflecting on someone's body language helps create a stronger sense of connection and rapport. It's about paying attention to their physical cues—like how they're sitting or leaning into the conversation—and mirroring those actions naturally and discreetly. For example, if they lean in, you lean in, too.

This approach has an impact because humans naturally tend to feel more comfortable with familiar surroundings. We instinctively gravitate toward people who seem like us, and that sense of sameness fosters trust and strengthens the bond.

The Link Between Healthy Relationships and Personal Development

Far too often, we look to our partners to heal us. I've been guilty of this myself, and chances are, you have, too, at some point in your life. But instead of finding the healing we seek, unresolved childhood wounds can work against us, slowly unraveling the relationship.

According to Harville Hendrix, the purpose of marriage isn't to search for the perfect spouse but to focus on personal growth and becoming a better companion. This can only happen when one enters a relationship equipped with the right tools, a clear understanding of the roots of one's emotional triggers, and a genuine willingness to grow and evolve.

He highlights the importance of personal growth and transformation in creating a fulfilling partnership. Imago therapy encourages partners to focus on self-reflection and take a closer look at their relationship dynamics to grow together. Helen LaKelly Hunt reinforces this idea, saying that relationships are where we uncover and step into our truest selves. She highlights how meaningful connections are essential for understanding who we are and for emotional and even physical healing. Imago therapy views relationships as more than just a connection—they're opportunities for personal and shared growth.

Using Imago Therapy to Heal and Strengthen Your Bonds

Before moving forward, sharing your intention with your partner is important. The process works so much better when both of you are on the same page and fully committed.

- Take a moment to reflect on your relationship and notice any recurring patterns, arguments, or emotional triggers. Think about how these patterns might be connected to your childhood experiences and the ways they've shaped you.

- Have intentional, meaningful conversations with your partner. Set aside time dedicated to connecting, free from phones, interruptions, rushing, and without distractions. Even the feeling of being short on time can hinder your ability to be present. Focus on using techniques like mirroring, validating, and empathizing to really understand each other and strengthen your connection.

- Create a safe and comfortable space to discuss sensitive topics. Ensure that you both feel heard, seen and appreciated throughout the conversation.

- Commit to growing both as individuals and as a couple by embracing a shared dedication to personal and relational development. Imago therapy strengthens your bond and supports healing childhood wounds, making it a powerful tool for personal growth. Understand that this kind of healing takes time and effort, so be patient with yourselves and with each other. Make it a priority to offer support and encouragement along the way, ensuring you're both cared for throughout the journey.

By embracing the principles of Imago therapy, you begin a journey of mutual healing and personal growth. Don't forget the process itself matters just as much as the outcome. With patience, empathy, and dedication, you can build a conscious, fulfilling relationship that supports each other and the world you create together.

Chapter 11:
Growth + Giving = Fulfillment

I'm here. I love you. I don't care if you need to stay up crying all night long; I will stay with you. If you need the medication again, go ahead and take it—I will love you through that, as well. If you don't need the medication, I will love you, too. There's nothing you can ever do to lose my love. I will protect you until you die, and after your death, I will still protect you. I am stronger than Depression, and I am braver than Loneliness, and nothing will ever exhaust me. –Elizabeth Gilbert

In *Eat Pray Love*, Elizabeth Gilbert invites us to join her as she dives deep into her heart, peeling back the layers to rediscover parts of herself she had lost along the way. Her journey wasn't just about traveling the globe—it was about coming home to herself in a real, raw, and wholehearted way. Elizabeth's triumphs that drew us in; it was the honesty of her struggles, fears, and moments of doubt. That's what made her story relatable. When you let people see who you really are—without the filters, without the bravado—that's when your glow becomes undeniable. It's about being true, and that kind of truth is magnetic.

Elizabeth's journey reminds you of who you are beneath the roles you play, the expectations you've carried, and the pain you've been holding onto. What Gilbert uncovered wasn't a brand-new version of herself—it was the light she'd buried under years of trying to live up to who she thought she needed to be.

When I talk about cultivating an inner glow, it's not about becoming some picture-perfect version of yourself that everyone admires. It's about letting go of the things that dim your light: the heavy expectations you've been carrying, the stories that have kept you stuck, and the armor you've built to protect yourself. You reconnect with who you are at your core and break through the barriers that have kept you stagnate. That glow isn't just some woo-woo idea; it's the energy that radiates when you decide to show up for yourself exactly as you are.

Your inner glow isn't about being the center of attention or the loudest voice in the room—it's about showing up as your truest self, radiating authenticity with every step you take. But life has a way of making us forget that, doesn't it? Everywhere we turn, there's a message telling us who we should be, how much we should accomplish, or why we're never quite enough as we are. Sometimes, it's an overwhelming roar; other times, it's a subtle whisper, always lingering in the background, nudging us to doubt ourselves.

In these moments, we face a choice: Do we let the noise define us, or do we turn it down and listen to our own voice instead? The pressure to measure up can dim our light, pulling us toward expectations and dreams that were never truly ours. But beneath it all—beneath the comparison, the striving, the self-doubt—your spark has always been there, waiting for you to return to it.

That glow gets buried underneath all the "should"s and "have-to"s that life piles on us. Reconnecting with it uncovers what's already inside you. It's about getting to the core of who you are and allowing yourself to get quiet enough to tune in with yourself. When you let go of the weight of trying to be who you think the world wants you to be, something magical happens—you feel lighter and freer, like you're finally coming home to yourself.

The journey to uncover it starts with something simple, yet so powerful—self-compassion.

Self-Compassion: Loving Yourself Through the Mess

Self-compassion is the soil where your inner glow begins to grow. It's about being there for yourself when things get messy, showing up with the same kindness you'd give to someone you love. The armor we wear so often comes from the fear that we're not enough. But when you meet yourself with grace, even in your hardest moments, you chip away at those hard edges. That's when your light starts to break through.

There's a profound freedom in choosing to love yourself. It's like finally letting out a deep exhale after holding your breath for far too long. You create space for your own humanity, and in that space, your radiance grows. It's about stepping into the vulnerable space of letting yourself be whole, even when you feel a little broken.

Achieving Happiness Through Growth

Growth is essential—it's what shapes who we are and who we're becoming. Every skill we master and every lesson we learn brings us closer to the person we want to be. Through this process, we build our self-worth and connect to the joy of transforming from the inside out. Fulfillment isn't about being perfect; it's about staying open to growth. That's what keeps us energized, grounded, and living a life that feels meaningful.

Fulfillment isn't a finish line you cross or a prize you win. Instead, it's an ever-evolving journey shaped by how you grow and the steps you take to better yourself. True fulfillment comes from the process—setting meaningful goals, facing challenges head-on, and uncovering new layers of who you are. In this constant pursuit of growth, a deeper, more lasting sense of contentment occurs.

Growing Beyond Constraints

To stay on track, having a clear personal development plan is key. Here's a simple exercise to help you get started:

1. Start by identifying areas in your life where you feel unfulfilled or see room for improvement. These could include physical health, career skills, emotional well-being, and personal relationships.

2. Once you've pinpointed these areas, set specific, measurable goals for each one. Dream big but keep your goals realistic and achievable to build momentum as you go.

3. Next, break your goals into actionable steps or milestones that lead you toward your vision. These smaller, manageable steps will help you tackle even the most intimidating goals confidently and clearly.

4. Check-in with yourself regularly to evaluate your progress and adjust your plan as needed. Life isn't static, and neither are you. Staying flexible ensures you keep moving forward, no matter how circumstances shift. By staying intentional and adaptable, you can transform even the most challenging areas of your life.

The Importance of Goal Setting

Goals give you clarity, purpose, and the motivation to move forward in life. The best goals should push you to grow and inspire you to keep going, but they should also feel achievable—not so overwhelming that you freeze before you start.

One effective way to set goals is by using the SMART framework:

- **Specific**: Be crystal clear about what you want to achieve. The more precise your goal, the easier it'll be to create a focused plan and track your progress.

- **Measurable**: Decide how you'll measure success. Clear metrics allow you to see where you're excelling and where adjustments are needed. Plus, celebrating small wins along the way keeps you motivated.

- **Achievable**: Set goals that challenge you but are still within reach. Aiming for the impossible often leads to frustration and disappointment, while realistic goals build confidence and momentum.

- **Relevant**: Make sure your goal aligns with your bigger life vision. Avoid getting caught up in checking off boxes just for the sake of it. Every goal should serve a meaningful purpose in your journey.

- **Time-bound**: Set a deadline to give yourself structure and accountability. Having a clear timeline helps keep you focused and on track.

This is your pathway to success and fulfillment—a chance to achieve your current goals and stay inspired for what's next. The goals you set should always align with your life's purpose, moving you closer to the vision you're working to create. If they don't, they become nothing more than a checklist; fulfillment isn't found in ticking boxes.

Finding Balance for Lasting Happiness

In today's fast-paced world, balancing work and personal life is essential for fulfillment. When work takes over, burnout creeps in, relationships suffer, and what brings us real joy gets left behind. The pressure to get everything *right* can feel overwhelming in this whirlwind of responsibilities. Finding balance is about prioritizing what matters and creating space for the life you want.

Against this tumultuous backdrop, the following words from Sadhguru bring some relief: "There is no such thing as work-life balance—it is all life. The balance must be within you." When we stop dwelling on past failures and allow ourselves to move forward, it's easier to focus and take the necessary steps to create balance.

Finding Your Balance

Finding balance allows you to thrive in your career without sacrificing your personal well-being. Even in this quest, there's guru wisdom we can learn from, "The simplest way to bring balance to your thoughts and emotions is an unwavering commitment towards something."

- Identify what you're committed to right now.

- How much time do you dedicate to both your work and personal life to honor this commitment?

- Take a close look at where you can make adjustments, whether it's setting stronger boundaries or carving out time for self-care, to better align with your commitment.

- Create a clear plan to implement these changes and make it a habit to check in with yourself regularly to evaluate your progress.

Achieving Fulfillment Through Contribution

Winston Churchill once said, "We make a living by what we get, but we make a life by what we give."

Abraham Maslow introduced the Hierarchy of Needs, a groundbreaking psychological theory on human motivation, in his 1943 paper *A Theory of Human Motivation*. Decades later, Tony Robbins built upon these principles with his Six Human Needs framework, making the concept more practical and accessible for personal growth and self-improvement. These six human needs are love and connection paired against significance, certainty paired with variety, and, once these are met, growth and contribution. The latter two are undeniably connected as growth feeds from contribution and *vice versa*.

Giving back—whether it's mentoring, volunteering, or showing kindness in small ways—adds meaning to our lives by connecting us to something bigger than ourselves.

This quote beautifully illustrates the transformative power of giving. When we share our time, talents, or resources to uplift others, we don't just impact their lives—we awaken a deeper sense of purpose within our own. True fulfillment isn't found in what we accumulate but in what we contribute. Giving back isn't just an act of kindness; it's a path to a richer, more meaningful life.

It's easy to believe we don't have much to offer, but that couldn't be further from the truth. Giving back doesn't have to be grand. It can be as simple as sharing your knowledge, lending a hand, or showing up for someone who needs support. Choose one way to make a difference and commit to it regularly. You'll soon realize that the impact isn't just on others, it's on you, too, bringing more meaning, purpose, and fulfillment into your own life.

We all have unique talents and strengths that make us who we are. Real fulfillment comes from discovering those gifts and finding ways to use them to make a difference. Think about the moments when you felt most alive and at peace—what were you doing? What strengths were you tapping into? These moments often reveal how you're naturally meant to contribute and leave your mark.

Shifting Focus for Greater Joy

Focusing too much on ourselves can make us stuck and dissatisfied. We overthink every conversation, replaying our words and actions, and become consumed by our own problems. We get so caught up in our own needs and struggles that we lose sight of what's happening around us. But shifting our attention outward—toward helping others and making a difference—can create a deeper sense of joy in our lives.

What if you made a deliberate effort to put someone else's needs ahead of your own? One way to practice compassion is by offering help or showing appreciation toward others. Notice how these small acts of kindness can brighten someone else's day while also leaving you feeling happier and more connected.

Creating Lasting Change

Growth and contribution create lasting fulfillment when they're woven into your daily life. Transformation is an ongoing process that takes consistent, intentional effort. The key is to take the behaviors and mindsets we've discussed and make them part of your everyday routine. Real, meaningful change that aligns with your values brings you closer to living your purpose.

By committing to self-improvement and positively affecting the world around you, you can lead a life rich with meaning, purpose, and happiness. Embrace growth and contribution, and you'll discover fulfillment that will last a lifetime.

Chapter 12:
Turning to Nature

The scariest part of ayahuasca, the thing that scares us the most, is that we might see ourselves. —Gerard Armond Powell

It's remarkable to think that something so ancient could offer solutions to challenges that even modern medicine struggles to overcome.

Here we are in the modern world, navigating life while carrying a quiet, relentless sense of unfulfillment—a shadow that lingers over everything we do. It's exhausting, heartbreaking even. But eventually, we all reach that breaking point, that rock bottom, where the suffering becomes too much to bear, and with every ounce of courage we have left, we say, "This is it. No more."

For me, that moment was perfectly aligned with my unexpected introduction to plant medicine.

I was at a casual barbecue with friends—a laid-back gathering of friends catching up and mingling with a few new faces when someone brought up ayahuasca.

My curiosity instantly ignited, like a door swinging open to something I hadn't even realized I was searching for. It's wild how a simple, offhand mention—just a passing remark—can set in motion a chain of events that would change my life. In plant medicine circles, they say ayahuasca calls you when you're ready. And in that moment, as I sat there hearing its name for the first time, I couldn't shake the feeling that it was calling me.

Ayahuasca is often described as a catalyst for spiritual awakening—a sacred, transformative experience sometimes referred to as "a pure secret." While it technically falls under the category of psychedelic drug, calling it a drug feels wildly inaccurate. Ayahuasca isn't something people take for fun, and using it'll hardly turn into an addiction. If anything, engaging with it requires a deep, unwavering commitment to breaking free from spiritual, mental, and emotional chains that are holding you back.

I remember coming across an article about Dr. Gabor Maté's use of ayahuasca to treat addiction. His words resonated so deeply that they never left me: "I sat there in the dark with my heart open and a feeling of delicious nurturing warmth, the tears of joy rolling down my face, and I got love. And I also learned how many ways in my life I have betrayed love and turned my back on it." Those words struck a chord because they reflected something I couldn't yet put into words myself.

By 2019, I found myself lost, struggling, and searching for answers in what I now know was my *Dark Night of the Soul.*

The Dark Night of the Soul

The term *Dark Night of the Soul* has its roots in the writings of Spanish mystic and poet St. John of the Cross, who captured the essence of the soul's struggle in darkness in his renowned poem of the same name. Written centuries ago, his words describe a profound sense of being lost, a deep spiritual and emotional darkness that many of us face at some point in life. The poem also speaks of the light—the divine light—that awaits on the other side. It's a reminder that when we endure the pain and push through the despair, we eventually emerge into something greater, into the light of God's love and grace.

Eckhart Tolle teaches us that the *Dark Night of the Soul* refers to a time of collapse of the meaning of life. Have you ever felt like your life suddenly lacked purpose? It's as if everything you once held onto suddenly feels empty, and you're pulled into an unfamiliar and deeply unsettling darkness. It's not just sadness— it's heavier, like a weight pressing down on your spirit. You yearn to break free from that suffocating shell and rediscover the light and purpose you once knew.

A single event can bring us to our knees, but more often, it's a series of moments—a slow erosion of certainty, a buildup of disappointments, or challenges stacking one after another—that breaks us down. It's rarely just one moment that makes us question everything: it's usually the weight of many, gradually chipping away at our sense of meaning.

This state is a time of transformation, when the old parts of you are stripped away to make space for something new to arise. It's the death of who you thought you were and the birth of who you're meant to become. The *Dark Night of the Soul* isn't just meaningless misery, it's the precursor to a spiritual awakening.

It was exactly that for me—a rebirth I didn't see coming but desperately needed.

My First Rendezvous with Ayahuasca

I dove headfirst into researching everything I could about this mystical healing tea.

This happened back in 2019, when ayahuasca remained largely unknown to many. For me, it was the beginning of a journey I never saw coming but one that I desperately needed.

Plant medicine has always carried a bit of stigma. Because of that, some people who've taken part in ceremonies choose to keep it private, worried about being judged or misunderstood. As I dug deeper, I learned that ayahuasca is a tea brewed from the leaves of one plant and the bark of another. It's not the kind of tea you sip for pleasure—the taste is very off-putting, but what it offers goes far beyond the physical realm.

Drinking it leads you into an intense spiritual journey, pulling you deep into your subconscious. It helps you uncover parts of yourself that you didn't even realize were hidden, forcing you to confront the barriers and blockages you've carried for years and, at times, even through generations. It's not an easy process, but one that allows you to release what no longer serves you and emerge into a space of light and clarity. It's as much about healing as it is about transformation—a journey that stays with you long after the ceremony is over.

The first time I heard the word *ayahuasca*, I was at one of the lowest points in my life. I felt hopeless, weighed down by a string of failed relationships. Deep down, I knew I was the common denominator. I couldn't ignore it anymore—I had to figure out what was blocking my heart. What was keeping love at bay? And perhaps even harder to face: What was stopping me from allowing myself to fully love in return?

I knew something had to give—I couldn't keep treading the same path and hoping for happiness to appear magically. That's when I took a leap of faith and booked a trip to *Rythmia*, a wellness center in Costa Rica. I'd heard it referred to as "Four Seasons of *Ayahuasca*," and as a solo female traveler, finding a place where I'd feel secure was non-negotiable. But I wasn't about to dive in without knowing what I was getting into. I spent weeks poring over information, reading everything I could find, and preparing myself for what lay ahead. In hindsight, that preparation wasn't just helpful—it was a crucial part of a journey.

The more I learned about *ayahuasca*, the more intrigued I became. Some claimed that a single session could be as powerful as 10 to 12 years of therapy. For me, therapy had always been sporadic— just a few sessions here and there—never anything consistent. But when I hit the point where I felt like I couldn't keep living the way I had been, when I realized I was in my own *Dark Night of the Soul*, I knew I needed something different. Anything.

Being in that space—completely consumed by despair—pushes you toward paths you never would have considered. I remember asking myself, *"What do you have to lose?"* And for the first time, the answer was undeniable: nothing.

Before leaving for Costa Rica, I had a few important steps to take in preparation. One of the biggest was adopting a vegan diet for two weeks—a purification process known as the *dieta*. The goal was to cleanse my body and align with my most authentic self before the experience. When I learned that consuming meat could mean absorbing the energy of the animals we eat, I knew that if I was going to do this, I had to fully commit.

Still, when I arrived at the wellness center, I couldn't help but think, "What am I doing? This is insane. Completely nuts!" It was a mix of excitement, nerves, and a touch of disbelief that I was there, about to embark on something so far outside my comfort zone.

I've always felt a pull toward spirituality—not religion. Growing up, my mom used to joke that I was a witch because I was always so captivated by the spiritual world. Even as a kid, I believed there was more to life than met the eye. I was the kind of child who would get caught up wondering why people have those little premonitions or moments of knowing that seem to come from nowhere.

When I arrived at *Rythmia*, the first thing on the schedule was a breathwork session. I'd never heard of breathwork before, so I had no idea what I was getting into. It turns out that breathwork uses specific breathing techniques to create a deep sense of inner peace. What really grabbed my attention was learning that this practice is rooted in neuroscience. By consciously controlling your breath, you can activate the vagus nerve, which is key to restoring calm in the body.

The vagus nerve, I learned, is the longest nerve in the body, and it controls essential functions like your heart rate, blood pressure, digestion, and breathing—all of which go haywire when you're stressed. Breathwork gives you the ability to "reset" by activating the vagus nerve, which in turn brings those systems back into balance. It blew my mind to think that something as simple as breathing could have such a profound impact. The idea was to work with your breath, intentionally changing your breathing patterns until you started feeling sensations or, at times, even seeing visions. I won't lie—it sounded wild to me at first. I had no idea what to expect. But as I got into it, its power completely blew me away.

As I settled into the rhythm, the visions began to unfold. Then, without warning, tears streamed down my face. It was overwhelming in the best way—a release I hadn't realized I needed. The experience was intense, raw, and deeply emotional, and all I could do was surrender to it. Holding back wasn't just impossible—it would have gone against everything this moment was meant to be.

By the end of that first night, so much of what I was experiencing made sense. Breathwork wasn't just powerful—it was transformative, setting the tone for everything that was to come.

That first night, many things started to come together. It felt like pieces of a puzzle were slowly clicking into place. But the real turning point came the following evening, the night of the first ayahuasca ceremony.

This was the moment I'd been preparing for. The night I'd been waiting for was finally here. I drank my first cup of *ayahuasca*. I learned it contains DMT, a compound with psychedelic properties that triggers a powerful reaction in the body. This reaction can lead to visions or *mental downloads*, which are known to carry deeply personal messages or insights meant for you.

I felt a mix of nerves and anticipation as I sat with the tea. They told us it could take anywhere from 20 to 40 minutes for the effects to kick in. Sitting there, waiting, I couldn't help but feel the weight of the moment. It was equally intimidating and exhilarating—not knowing what was about to happen. In this altered state of consciousness, I sat in the *maloca* (a large communal house traditionally used by indigenous people). It serves as a multi-purpose structure that is central to the community's social, cultural, and spiritual life.

There I was, sitting in a room full of strangers. I was surrounded by people from every corner of the world—people of different ages, religions, and walks of life—all gathered for this shared experience. The *shaman* (A shaman is a spiritual guide and healer who acts as a bridge between the physical and spiritual realms) and helpers moved quietly throughout the room, ensuring everyone felt safe as the *ayahuasca* began to take effect.

I found myself sitting next to a girl I hadn't met. At some point, she got up to go to the restroom. I didn't think much of it. By then, I started feeling cold and moved to another area. I gathered my things, relocated to a different section of the room, and decided I should probably use the restroom as well before the ceremony. When I came back and sat down, I looked over and realized I was sitting next to the same girl again. "This is so strange," I said. "Did you notice I moved?" She looked just as puzzled as I felt and replied, "No, I was in the bathroom." It was such a small, seemingly coincidental moment, but before the ceremony began, we were told that whatever happens under the *maloca* is for a reason.

I thought to myself, this isn't a coincidence. We're meant to sit next to each other for some reason. It felt like one of those odd synchronicities that made you pause and wonder about the deeper meaning behind it. At this point, it was me, the girl I'd just met, and then another girl from Australia, sitting close to one another. We all chit-chatted for a bit and became friendly. About half an hour later, the girl who moved and was next to me started having a visceral reaction.

My first thought (typical New Yorker) was, 'This is going to be annoying.'

She kept having these intense, almost uncontrollable reactions— kicking and writhing—which I knew was something that could happen during this experience. We were told not to talk or interact with anyone during the ceremony, so I just sat there, completely distracted. It got to the point where I felt like I couldn't focus on anything else. I wanted to leave. But I stayed, reminding myself of what we'd been told: no matter what happens, don't leave the *maloca*, the real healing and transformation happens under the *maloca*.

I glanced over at an Australian girl nearby, wondering how she was doing, even feeling a sense of concern for her. But then it hit me—someone sitting right next to me was having their own visible reaction, and instead of feeling compassion, I just felt irritated. The contrast was striking. It was a sudden realization that caught me off guard.

I thought to myself, 'Why am I so annoyed by her? Why don't I feel the same compassion and concern for her that I feel for the other girl?' That contrast stopped me in my tracks. It was like a mirror was being held up, forcing me to confront something deep within myself. 'Why doesn't her struggle evoke the same empathy?'

It wasn't my finest moment, but it taught me more about myself than I could've anticipated. As I sat there, my thoughts unraveled. I realized that I saw people who needed help as weak. And that realization didn't sit well with me. 'Why does it bother me so much?' I don't want to view people in need as weak. We all have moments of vulnerability and weaknesses. She was just having hers now, and I wasn't. That didn't make her weak—it made her human.

I realized I should care more about her well-being, but instead I was shutting down. 'Why am I like this? Why am I so closed off?' I didn't want to be this person anymore. It was like staring into a mirror and seeing a side of myself I didn't like. I felt like a bully. I don't want to be a bully, I thought. I want to be helpful. I want to be kind. I want to be a good person.

The moment that realization hit, I started vomiting, or what is known as purging. Purging occurs during *shamanic* rituals, such as *ayahuasca* ceremonies. In this context, it's a physical or emotional release that participants experience as part of their healing journey. Forms of purging can be vomiting, crying, sweating, laughing, shaking, and for some, even defecation.

Purging is said to be a good thing. It's your body's way of releasing all the toxicity and negativity you've been holding on to. I couldn't stop. I kept purging, repeatedly, with all these strange sounds coming out of me. It was overwhelming and surreal, but at that moment, I knew something inside me was shifting.

I understood something extremely important at that moment: my heart had been closed off. That realization was my first true *aha* moment—a turning point that showed me just how much work I had to do.

I then experienced another profound download. This time, it was about my nephew. I suddenly understood why I love him so deeply: he was the first person I ever felt unconditional love from. That realization hit me hard.

I often found myself wondering, *"Why am I so deeply attached to this child?"* Other people didn't seem to have such an intense connection with their nieces or nephews. But then it hit me—it wasn't just about him. It was about what his love unlocked in me. His love opened my heart in a way I had never allowed myself to experience before. It showed me what it felt like to be truly, unconditionally loved. Not that my parents didn't love me—they did—but his love made me feel seen. It was so pure, so free of conditions, that for the first time, I believed I was lovable. That I was worthy of love in its most honest and unfiltered form.

Ayahuasca can convey visions. I saw my mother. She was only 22 when she had me, so young and unsure of the path ahead. I saw her and my dad together in a room with me as a baby. I could feel their fear, their uncertainty, and their love all at once. For the first time, I could see them as people, not just as parents, and it gave me a perspective I never knew I needed.

I realized my parents were essentially kids themselves when they had me—just two young adults trying to figure it all out, barely knowing themselves, let alone how to raise a newborn child. I thought about myself at that age, and how unprepared and lost I would've been if I'd had a child so young. That perspective shifted something deep within me. For the first time in my life, I was ready to finally forgive them.

In a single session, my relationship with my parents changed. I forgave my dad for his indiscretions. I forgave my mom for her lack of emotional support and vulnerability. I saw them for what they were—just humans raising another human. We tend to put our parents on pedestals, expecting them to be superheroes, and when they fall short, we judge them harshly. But that night, I saw them as people—flawed, like we all are, and doing their best with what they had.

That *ayahuasca* journey spanned four nights, each one peeling back another layer.

What I Learned from This Experience

At first, my experience was subtle, but by the third or fourth evening, something shifted. As I sank into a deeper state of awareness, a profound truth revealed itself: Ayahuasca doesn't give you what you want—it gives you what you *need*. To experience its power, you must be willing to surrender. Open yourself up, become vulnerable, and trust the process, even when it feels uncertain and uncomfortable.

The key is letting go of control and allowing Mother Ayahuasca to guide. It's in that surrender, in that willingness to flow with the experience, that the real transformation happens. And once you embrace it, the freedom and insight it brings is unlike anything else.

Why is it often referred to as Mother Ayahuasca? Because *ayahuasca* embodies the pure, unconditional love we're all born with but often lose sight throughout our lives. When you let go, step into vulnerability, and stop resisting its power, you're enveloped in a profound love that feels deeply maternal. That's the essence of Mother Ayahuasca: a love that nurtures and heals.

Of course, something this powerful comes with important health and safety precautions. You can't take *ayahuasca* if you're on certain medications, especially SSRIs, as it can trigger dangerous medical complications. This isn't something to approach casually—it demands careful preparation and respect.

The experience itself is far from easy. After drinking ayahuasca, you might feel nothing at first. But then, after about 45 minutes, a wave of deep relaxation sets in. Then comes the purging—yes, the vomiting. It's not because the tea makes you physically sick; science has shown that. The purging is spiritual, a way of clearing the toxic emotions, blockages, and darkness you've been carrying. It's intense and challenging but also profoundly cleansing, making space for something more authentic to ascend.

The Lone Path to Growth

Finding a trusted, reputable shaman is essential for an experience of that magnitude. The ceremony must be conducted in a space of safety and support.

My advice? Go alone. Friends have asked to join me or mentioned they'd like to come along the next time I sit in ceremony, but I always politely decline. It's human nature to worry about the people we care about, and when someone close to you is there, it's easy to become distracted by their experience. If you're an empath, their emotions or energy can pull you out of your own journey, keeping you from fully diving into your subconscious. This is an intensely personal process, and going solo allows you to surrender completely without outside interference. As daunting as it may seem, trust me—it's worth it.

Read up on the safety protocols of the retreat or *shaman* you choose. While problems are rare, *ayahuasca* affects everyone differently, and things can go wrong. It's crucial to know you're surrounded by people who are trained to handle any situation that might occur.

Integration can be just as important as sitting with the medicine. After the ceremony, talk to someone who understands what you've been through. Sharing your experience with someone who gets it can help you process everything and make sense of what you've just experienced. It can also help you integrate those lessons into your life in a meaningful way.

If you feel called to explore *ayahuasca*, start by doing your research. Speak to people with experience with the medicine; learn as much as you can about what to expect. You don't have to dive in right away. Even attending a *shamanic* ceremony without taking the medicine can be a powerful first step and a way to ease into the experience.

Tepezcohuite

Tepezcohuite is another powerful form of plant medicine that can help you overcome emotional and mental barriers. Unlike *ayahuasca*, which is brewed into tea, *tepezcohuite* is smoked. The experience is similar in depth but much shorter—usually lasting only 10 to 15 minutes compared to *ayahuasca's* 4 to 6 hours. Because it happens so quickly, the intensity is amplified, making it an incredibly profound yet concentrated journey.

This intensity means you'll likely spend significant time after the ceremony processing what you've just experienced, dissecting the meaning of your visions and downloads. The clarity and insight it brings often require careful reflection to integrate.

Tepezcohuite, known as the Tree of Life, comes from Mayan tradition and is considered safe when used correctly. It's often called the Mayan version of *ayahuasca*, but it works in its own unique way. Tepezcohuite targets and dismantles larger, more deeply ingrained mental and emotional blocks. It's not a casual experience, but for those ready to deep dive, it offers transformative breakthroughs that are as intense as they are life changing.

Is Plant Medicine the Solution for Everybody?

While I believe everyone can benefit from plant medicine, I don't think everyone is ready for it. Approaching it without being prepared can feel overwhelming, even frightening. Instead of being a natural, intuitive process, it can feel forced—and that's the wrong way to experience it.

I wholeheartedly believe that everyone should learn about plant medicine. Breaking the stigma around it starts with awareness. People need to understand that it's a powerful tool for healing emotional pain and distress, not something to be feared or dismissed. These plants are gifts from the Earth, and we all deserve the chance to explore their potential when we feel called to.

Educating yourself about plant medicine doesn't just open your mind to its possibilities—it also helps you better understand the blockages you might be carrying. It's easy to go through life without ever acknowledging our blockages; many people do. But if you're reading this book, I don't think you are one of those people. As long as these blockages remain buried and unacknowledged, they'll continue to weigh you down, limiting your ability to live authentically.

Often, these blockages prevent you from stepping into vulnerability. They're how you maintain your armor and keep love at a distance. They serve as a defense, but they also shut out some of life's most meaningful experiences.

We're standing at the edge of a plant-medicine and psychedelic renaissance, where these ancient tools are finally being rediscovered and embraced for their power to heal, transform, and reconnect us with our truest selves.

Getting Practical: Identifying Spiritual Blockages

Even if you aren't drawn to plant medicine, exploring and understanding the blockages that keep you feeling stuck can still be incredibly beneficial. The walls we build around our hearts don't disappear on their own, but gaining clarity is the first step toward freedom.

Start by giving yourself space to simply *be* rather than constantly *do*.

Use this time to check in with yourself. Ask questions like:

- Am I feeling miserable, stressed, exhausted, or even depressed?

- Does life feel unusually difficult, as though I'm exerting far more effort just to keep up?

- Is my body hypersensitive to light, sound, or the chaos around me?

- Am I struggling to focus or having difficulty remembering new information?

These could be signs of emotional, mental, or spiritual blockages holding you back from living fully. While plant medicine can offer powerful breakthroughs, it's not the only way to dismantle these walls.

By carving out time for reflection and stillness, you can reconnect with yourself and identify what's weighing you down. These small, intentional steps can help you move closer to the freedom and clarity you're seeking.

Part III:
Soft Armor in Action

Chapter 13:
Rewire for Positivity

Positive thinking will let you do everything better than negative thinking will. —Zig Ziglar

Have you ever walked into a room and instantly felt the energy shift? One moment, you're fine, and the next, a wave of heaviness, anxiety, or irritation takes over—without explanation. It's as if someone else's tension or bad mood has silently seeped into your own. I've seen this happen countless times, especially in high-pressure team environments.

I remember standing in line at the airport, waiting to go through security. The mood was neutral, people scrolling through their phones, chatting quietly, lost in their own thoughts. Then, a frustrated traveler stormed in, sighing loudly, muttering complaints under their breath, and aggressively shifting their weight as if the entire process was a personal inconvenience. The shift was instant. The people around them tensed. Conversations stalled. Even the TSA agents seemed less patient. It was a powerful reminder that energy is contagious—we don't just experience it, we spread it.

Emotions are complex psychophysiological responses that significantly influence our thoughts and behaviors. While emotions themselves aren't energy waves with measurable frequencies, they do produce physiological changes in the body that can be quantified. For instance, emotional arousal often leads to an increase in heart rate and blood pressure. These changes are mediated by the autonomic nervous system, which governs involuntary bodily functions. Researchers utilize various tools to measure these physiological responses, providing insights into how different emotions manifest physically. For example, studies have shown that emotions like fear and anger can increase heart rate and blood pressure, while sadness may lead to decreased heart rate. These measurable changes help scientists understand the intricate relationship between emotional experiences and bodily responses (Bauer RM. Physiologic measures of emotion).

When you're in a bad mood, the energy you project is completely different from someone who's feeling happy and at ease. When these opposing energies collide, they don't just coexist—they clash. And often, negativity takes the upper hand, disrupting the balance. It's why one person's bad mood can shift the entire atmosphere of a room, pulling everyone into its orbit.

The energy we project—whether positive or negative—can impact those around us from nearly ten feet away, without saying a word. Realizing this completely shifted my perspective on group dynamics. We're all carrying our own emotional weight, and the last thing we need is to absorb someone else's negativity.

So, how do you reset when someone else's bad energy clings to you like static? How do you shake it off and protect your peace?

Recognize and Own Your Emotions

Whether the negativity is coming from someone else or simmering within you, the first step is to acknowledge it. In the corporate world, I've seen how unchecked stress can snowball, dragging entire teams down from high-performing to completely burnt out. It happens not because people lack talent or drive, but because no one stops to check in with their own energy. It's tough to watch, but it's also a reminder: the energy you bring matters. When you take ownership of how you feel, you regain the power to change it.

You can't always control what's happening around you, but you can control how you respond. If you're carrying frustration, acknowledge it. Check in with yourself and ask, *what energy am I bringing into this moment? How can I shift it in a way that serves me and those around me?* This isn't just about feeling better—it's about leading with intention and showing up in a way that has a positive impact.

But here's the tricky part: how do you protect your energy without shutting out the good? How do you stay open without letting negativity drain you? It's not easy, but learning to walk that line is what allows you to move from simply getting by to thriving.

The Neuroscience of Positivity

You build a positive mindset by training your brain to lean in that direction. Choosing positivity doesn't mean your life will suddenly be free of challenges, and it doesn't solve all your problems overnight. Instead, it changes the way you approach those challenges. It opens you up to new perspectives, helping you see possibilities and solutions that might've been hidden in plain sight.

Positivity has a ripple effect. It gives you resilience, helps you bounce back faster, and creates a magnetic energy that draws people in. But let's not sugarcoat things—life can hit hard, and staying hopeful during difficult times can feel like an uphill battle. The good news? You don't have to force it. Once your mind adapts to seeing the world through a more optimistic perspective, it becomes automatic, it becomes something you don't have to consciously work at anymore.

So, how do you rewire your brain for positivity? It starts with understanding how adaptable your brain really is. Remember the concept of neuroplasticity from Chapter 1? Neuroplasticity is the brain's ability to change and form new pathways throughout your life. By consistently practicing new ways of thinking and behaving, you're not just shifting your mindset; you're physically changing the structure of your brain. And over time, positivity becomes less of a practice and more of a way of being.

We all can reshape our brains and train them to adopt a more positive outlook. When you consistently focus on the good— whether it's appreciating small joys, celebrating wins, or counting your blessings—you strengthen the brain's pathways for positivity while naturally quieting the ones tied to pessimism. Our brains are wired to grow and adapt, but here's the key: You're in charge of navigation that growth. Do you lean toward positivity or let negativity take the lead?

Dr. Michael Merzenich, a pioneer in the field of neuroplasticity, explains: "Your brain is not fixed. It's adaptable. It'll be shaped and reshaped continuously by the things you do, the things you think, and by the environments you live in." The challenge is remembering that you can't let outside circumstances dictate your mindset. That control belongs to you. Taking ownership of your brain's development means guiding it intentionally through consistent practices. It's about showing up, day by day, and creating a mental framework that supports the life you want.

Cognitive Reappraisal: Transforming Your Emotional Responses

Cognitive reappraisal is a powerful technique for managing emotions. Instead of suppressing negative feelings, it encourages you to reinterpret a situation to change its emotional impact. For example, viewing a challenging event as a learning opportunity can reduce stress and improve well-being.

Scientific studies support this approach. Research indicates that cognitive reappraisal activates the prefrontal cortex, which is involved in thinking and decision-making, it reduces activity in the amygdala, the brain's fear center. This shift helps decrease feelings of anxiety and depression. Regularly practicing this technique can enhance emotional resilience and overall mental health. It demonstrates that while you can't always control what happens, you can control your response.

Unlocking the Superpower of Your Mind

The next time you're in a frustrating situation, like missing the bus or subway, try reframing your thoughts. It's so easy to slip into thinking, 'This is such a waste of time,' and feel your mood spiral into frustration. But what if you took a different perspective? Instead, you could think, 'This is a chance to finally listen to that podcast or audiobook I've been wanting to check out.' That small mental shift can completely change how you feel.

Focus dictates perception.

Where you choose to focus your attention has a massive impact on how you experience life. For example, dwelling on an empty bank account won't make you any poorer, but it *will* amplify feelings of scarcity. Meanwhile, focusing on the things you *do* have won't magically add zeros to your balance, but it'll shift how you feel about your situation. When you constantly focus on what's missing, your brain doesn't just notice it—it reinforces it. Over time, your thoughts, actions, and even the way you interpret the world start to align with that mindset, keeping you stuck in the same cycle.

This happens because of something called *selective attention*. Your brain filters information based on what you believe is important. If you're always looking for what's wrong, your mind will find more reasons to confirm it, creating a self-fulfilling prophecy. But the opposite is also true—when you start appreciating the good, your brain adapts, making it easier to see more of what's working in your life.

The Impact of Language

Words are powerful because they carry an energy that impact our thoughts and feelings. Think about how a great speech or a heartfelt song can instantly change your mood—it's almost like magic. The same applies to the words we use in our daily lives. The language you choose to describe yourself and your experiences directly impacts your mindset. Positive words can encourage you, making challenges feel less overwhelming. On the flip side, negative words can pull you down, undermining your confidence and limiting your belief in what you can achieve.

This doesn't just apply to what you say out loud. Your inner dialogue—the words you say to yourself—matters just as much. Positive self-talk can strengthen your conviction in your abilities, while negative self-talk can hold you back in ways you might not realize. The best part? You have the power to change this. It starts with being mindful of the words you use in conversations and your thoughts. Once you recognize the patterns, you can begin replacing limiting language with words that empower you. Over time, this simple practice rewires your mindset, helping you build a stronger, more resilient outlook on life.

Positive Exposure Therapy: Reconditioning Emotional Responses

Exposure therapy is traditionally used to help people face and overcome their fears by gradually exposing them to what makes them anxious in a safe, controlled environment. Instead of focusing on fears, you can intentionally expose yourself to positive experiences and influences that help neutralize negative emotional responses. Over time, this deliberate practice can rewire your brain, making it easier to approach life with a more optimistic and resilient mindset.

Published research confirms that imagery rescripting, where individuals mentally reimagine distressing memories in a more positive or adaptive way, can significantly reduce the emotional impact of negative memories (Simon et al., 2024). Participants who practiced this technique experienced less emotional distress and reported improvements in their resilience and emotional well-being.

Using Practical Exposure Therapy to Improve Your Mood

Working with a trained professional is a great way to dive deeper into the practice, but there are also simple techniques you can try on your own.

- Start by pinpointing situations or memories that stir up negative emotions.

- Once you've identified your triggers, try gradually exposing yourself to positive influences tied to those experiences. This could be something as simple as revisiting a happy memory, looking at images that make you smile, or doing something you love that feels connected to the moment.

- This approach can help neutralize negative feelings over time with consistency. It's about retraining your brain and creating a healthier, more positive way of responding to the things that once held you back.

Novelty-Seeking

Trying new experiences is a surprisingly powerful way to rewire your brain. Each time you step out of your routine, your brain releases dopamine. But it's not just about instant gratification. New activities and skills also spark creativity and help you stay mentally flexible, opening the door to fresh perspectives and a greater sense of joy.

Incorporating novelty into your daily life doesn't have to be a big production. Start small. Take a different route to work, try a food you've never had, or sign up for a class that interests you. Little changes can make a big difference. The goal is to keep your brain engaged and curious. Over time, these simple shifts can promote growth, boost positivity, and help you approach life with a renewed sense of adventure.

Curating Your Mental Diet

Just as the food you eat shapes your physical health, the media you consume influences your mental well-being. Every article you read, every show you watch, and every scroll through social media leaves an imprint. Being intentional about what you engage with can make a profound difference. Choose content that uplifts and inspires rather than drains or overwhelms you. When you become mindful of what you allow into your mental space, you take back control over your mindset and emotional state.

Here's something to keep in mind: once you see something, you can't unsee it. Before engaging, ask yourself, *Do I really want this taking up space in my mind?* Let that question be your filter, especially when it comes to content that feels draining or unsettling.

Switching to a more positive media diet can profoundly affect your mental health. When you surround yourself with content that nourishes your mind and spirit, you'll find it easier to stay balanced, focused, and connected to what matters in your life.

Getting Practical About Social Media Consumption

Reprogramming your mindset toward positivity takes consistent effort, but the rewards are well worth it. Practices like gratitude, positive affirmations, visualization, cognitive reframing, and increased consciousness are powerful tools that can reshape your outlook and improve your overall well-being. The key is to remind yourself that you can change your thoughts—and by doing so, you can change your life. Integrating these practices into your daily routine will make you feel more optimistic, fulfilled, and at peace.

One simple but impactful step is to evaluate how you consume media.

- Pay attention to where you spend your time and what kind of content you engage with. Is it inspiring, or is it draining and stressful?

- Consider prioritizing media that adds value to your day— things that educate, motivate, or bring you joy.

- Limit your exposure to negative news, social media conflicts, and anything that weighs on your mental space.

Every small step you take reinforces your brain's natural ability to grow and adapt. Over time, you'll notice the cumulative effects: greater happiness, resilience, and a deeper sense of purpose. The journey of mental transformation is a process, but as you commit to it, you will see how even the smallest choices can lead to big changes in your outlook and your life.

Chapter 14:
Bouncing Back

Resilience isn't just about bouncing back; it's about bouncing forward.
Use setbacks as stepping stones to propel you toward your goals.
—David Goggins

Life is a journey consisting of high peaks and low valleys, where triumphs and challenges coexist. But it's not the challenges that shape us—it's how we respond to them. Life isn't neatly categorized as hard or easy, good or bad. It's a canvas, and how we choose to see it becomes the art we create.

Picture two people encountering the same challenge. One feels weighed down by it, while the other sees it as a chance to grow, adapt, and become stronger. The challenge doesn't change—but their perspective does, and that perspective is what determines the outcome.

Resilience is more than just bouncing back; it's about finding joy and meaning even when life gets difficult. It's the ability to recover from setbacks, adapt to new realities, and keep moving forward with faith and flexibility. The more resilient you are, the stronger you rise after every fall. Hitting rock bottom doesn't have to break you—it can build you. And with every comeback, you become more seasoned, powerful, and prepared to face whatever lies ahead.

Resilience has been my anchor. I can still remember the nights when the weight of sadness felt unbearable, the days when loneliness echoed so loudly it seemed inescapable. But resilience isn't about always feeling strong or having all the answers—it's about choosing to take one more step, even when it feels impossible, and trusting that brighter days are ahead.

It's what brought me to where I am today. I can now guide others through their struggles, not from a place of theory but from experience. I learned that there's space for healing and growth, even in the depths of doubt and pain. It's not about waiting for the light at the end of the tunnel—it's about creating your own light, one flicker at a time. That's the magic of resilience: it doesn't just help you survive; it transforms you into someone stronger, wiser, who can rise again and again no matter what happens.

Tapping into resilience can feel overwhelming because it means confronting your pain head-on—something that's never easy. It's human nature to avoid discomfort, to hope that if we ignore the hard stuff, it will somehow fade away. But it doesn't. It lingers, waiting. Resilience isn't about avoidance; it's about stepping into the discomfort, facing the struggle, and trusting that in doing so, you'll be stronger.

Is it scary? Without a doubt. Vulnerability is uncomfortable, and the fear of failure can make you want to hide. But here's the truth: resilience isn't just about enduring hardship—it's about rising through it. It's about using adversity as fuel, transforming challenges into stepping stones rather than roadblocks.

Now is the perfect time to explore the strategies that make resilience possible and transformative. Let's dive into the mindset shifts that help you navigate life's storms with grace, courage, and unshakable confidence.

Few quotes capture the heart of resilience—the uphill battles it demands and the life-changing rewards it delivers—like the iconic speech by Theodor Roosevelt, *The Man in the Arena*:

> "It is not the critic who counts; not the man who points out how the strong man stumbles, or where the doer of deeds could have done them better. The credit belongs to the man who is actually in the arena, whose face is marred by dust and sweat and blood; who strives valiantly, who errs; who comes short again and again, because there is no effort without error and shortcoming; but who does actually strive to do the deeds; who knows great enthusiasms, the great devotions; who spends himself in a worthy cause; who at the best knows in the end the triumph of high achievement, and who at the worst, if he fails, at least fails while daring greatly, so that his place shall never be with those cold and timid souls who neither know victory nor defeat."

Roosevelt's speech isn't only about bravery but the grit it takes to get back up when you're down. It's not easy. It demands persistence, adaptability, and the courage to face the risk of falling again. And that's where it gets real: being in the arena is raw and vulnerable, and it's where resilience is truly put to the test.

Resilient people possess the mental and emotional strength to push forward, even when the weight of life feels overwhelming.

It's about adapting, growing, and choosing to show up for yourself—especially when things get messy.

The Psychological Foundations of Resilience

Resilience comes down to a few core principles that help you handle life's unexpected curveballs with a positive, adaptable mindset.

1. **Optimism:** Resilient people are good at finding the silver lining, even when life feels impossible. They believe they can influence outcomes and make meaning out of even the toughest situations. It's not about ignoring reality—it's about choosing hope.

2. **Emotional regulation:** Emotions can be messy, but resilience is about creating space for them without letting them take control. It's about pausing, acknowledging what you feel, and allowing those emotions to move through you—without letting them define you. It's the ability to say, *"I feel this, but it doesn't own me.*

3. **Self-efficacy:** This is your inner *"I've got this"* voice—the belief that no matter what comes your way, you'll find a way through. When you trust in your ability to figure things out, challenges feel less like roadblocks and more like opportunities to grow. Self-efficacy fuels your confidence, keeps you moving forward, and shifts your focus from problems to solutions.

4. **Cognitive flexibility:** This is your inner *"I've got this"* voice—the deep trust in your ability to navigate challenges as they come. When you believe in yourself, setbacks feel less like barriers and more like problems waiting to be

solved. Self-efficacy fuels your confidence, keeps you moving forward and shifts your focus from obstacles to opportunities.

The Crucial Components of Resilience

Resilient people don't just endure challenges—they grow from them. They've cultivated a mindset that views setbacks not as roadblocks, but as opportunities to learn and adapt. That shift in perspective is what allows them to rise stronger after every fall.

Resilience is built on five key pillars:

1. **Positive Mindset**: When confronted by challenges, ask, "What can I take away from this?" Resilient people know that even the hardest moments can teach them something valuable.

2. **Strong Relationships**: Resilient people lean on their support system, whether that's family, friends, or coworkers. They know when to ask for help and value the advice, perspective, and strength others can provide.

3. **Adaptability**: Change is inevitable, and resilience is about rolling with it. Resilient people stay flexible, open-minded, and ready to shift gears when necessary. If one approach doesn't work, they're not afraid to try something new.

4. **Purpose and Meaning**: Having a clear "why" keeps you grounded. Resilient people find meaning in their struggles. They know their challenges aren't pointless; they're part of a bigger journey toward their goals. That sense of purpose keeps them going, no matter how hard things get.

The Benefits of Resilience

1. **Better Mental Health**: Resilience is like armor against stress, anxiety, and even depression. Instead of getting stuck in the weight of challenges, resilient people manage and move through them. That ability to keep steady helps protect their mental and emotional well-being.

2. **Smarter Problem-Solving**: Stress can cloud your thinking and make problems seem impossible. Resilient people can stay calm and focused, approaching challenges with a solutions-first mindset. They don't let problems overwhelm them but instead, find creative ways to work through whatever's in front of them.

3. **A More Fulfilling Life**: Resilient people lead happier, more satisfying lives. They know how to navigate adversity with purpose, optimism, and an understanding that every experience—good or bad—has something to teach them. Even when they don't "win," they never walk away empty-handed.

4. **Stronger Relationships**: Resilience strengthens connections with others. Resilient people know how to communicate openly, ask for support, and offer it in return. These qualities build trust and deepen relationships over time.

Getting Practical in Flexing Your Resilience Muscle

You build resilience bit by bit. It grows over time with experience, reflection, and practice. Every time life knocks you down, and you get back up, you strengthen that muscle.

Practice Self-Compassion

When life gets tough, give yourself grace. Seriously—don't add unnecessary pressure. Setbacks are inevitable; they're part of the journey. While you can't always control what happens, you *can* choose how you respond. Will you let obstacles keep you down, or will you use them as fuel to rise even stronger? The choice is yours.

Write yourself a letter. Pretend you're writing to your best friend who's struggling. What would you say? You'd tell them it's okay to struggle, that they're doing their best, and that they'll be okay. Now, give yourself that same love and encouragement. You deserve it just as much.

Build a Support Network

Surround yourself with the people who truly support you—the ones who lift you up when you're struggling and bring clarity when life feels chaotic. Maybe it's someone who listens without judgment, offers honest advice, or simply keeps you accountable. The right people in your corner don't just make life easier; they make you stronger.

Take a moment to think about the people who truly have your back. Write down the friends, family members, or mentors you trust most—the ones you can turn to when you need extra support. And don't be afraid to lean on them. That's what they're there for. You were never meant to carry it all alone.

Maintain Physical Health

Regular exercise, eating well, and getting enough sleep aren't just good for your health—they directly affect how you handle stress and improve your outlook. Everything else feels a little easier to manage when your body feels good.

A quick walk, some light stretching, or even just getting up and moving around can work wonders for your mood and energy.

The foundation? Strengthen your mindset, surround yourself with the right people, and learn to view obstacles as opportunities for growth. Like any skill, resilience builds over time—the more you practice, the better you become at navigating challenges and coming out stronger on the other side.

As you continue your journey, remember the words of Winston Churchill: "Success is not final, failure is not fatal: it's the courage to continue that count."

Chapter 15:
Radiate Charisma

"Charismatic behavior can be broken down into three core elements: presence, power, and warmth." - Olivia Fox Cabane

I think I found my charisma when I stopped trying to fit into the mold of what I thought others wanted from me and allowed myself to be exactly who I am—fully and unapologetically. That shift changed everything. People started connecting with me on a deeper level, not because I was trying to impress them, but because I was showing up as myself, without pretense or hesitation. Authenticity has a quiet magnetism—it doesn't chase approval, yet it naturally draws people in.

For me, charisma is a mix of what's seen and what's felt—something you can recognize but can't always put into words. It's in the way someone carries themselves, the way they listen, the energy they bring into a room. I notice it in those moments when conversation flows effortlessly, when someone's presence makes you feel at ease, or when a connection forms without force or effort. There's a natural pull, a sense of trust that doesn't need to be explained. But charisma isn't something you can fake or rehearse—it's an energy that comes from being fully comfortable with who you are. It's about owning your space, speaking with intention, and letting your presence do the rest. That's what makes it unforgettable.

I don't think charisma is something you're just born with. It's something you develop when you start to really get to know yourself—when you do the inner work, heal, and step fully into your truth. That's when the magic happens. People are drawn to authenticity, and to me, that's what charisma is all about. It's not about being the loudest in the room or having all the answers— it's about being so comfortable in your own skin that others feel that comfort, too.

That's how I've come to see and grow my own charisma. It's not some mystical quality reserved for a select few. Anyone can cultivate it. The more naturally magnetic you become, the more you lean into your truth and own who you are.

Charisma is really about connection—making people feel seen, heard, and valued. It elevates everything, from how you show up in your personal life to how you thrive professionally.

The Elements of Charisma

Charismatic people have an energy about them that's hard to ignore. They're confident because they know their worth. When someone believes in themselves with that much conviction, it's contagious. You just automatically feel better being around them.

Empathy is at the heart of their charm. Charismatic people don't just listen—they *tune in*. They don't simply hear your words; they understand you. They genuinely care about what you're feeling and what you have to say, creating a connection that builds trust.

You walk away from the conversation not just heard, but seen and understood.

Authenticity is everything. The most magnetic people don't try to be anything other than themselves—genuine, honest, and unapologetically real. Their sincerity creates a sense of ease, making others feel comfortable and naturally drawn to them.

And then there's their presence. You know, those people who make you feel like you're the only person in the room when they're talking to you. Charismatic people are fully engaged with you. They're not distracted or looking for the next conversation—they're completely engaged, making you feel significant.

Finally, they know how to express themselves. It's in their tone, gestures, and even how they tell a story. They bring their words to life in a natural and captivating way.

The Benefits of Having Charisma

Charisma makes it easier to build strong, meaningful connections. It creates a sense of trust, respect, and understanding that makes interactions—both personal and professional—feel more natural and engaging. When someone has that kind of energy, people can't help but be drawn to them. It's not something that needs to be forced—it just flows.

Charisma is a game-changer in leadership, too. Charismatic leaders have a way of lighting a fire in the people around them. They don't just manage—they connect. Their ability to communicate clearly and form genuine relationships gives them an edge, whether they're leading a team or running an entire company. It's not just about influence; it's about inspiring trust and making decisions people believe in.

Charisma makes networking feel effortless. Some people just have a vibe that naturally draws others in without trying too hard. It's not about working the room or putting on a show. It's more like their energy creates this magnetism that opens doors to genuine connections and unexpected opportunities.

When it's authentic, charisma is about lifting people up—not using them. They inspire growth and help people step into their own potential. That's what makes true charisma so rare—it's not just about being likable. It's about integrity, empathy, and a genuine desire to leave people better than how you found them.

According to John Maxwell, a well-known authority on leadership, people may be able to hear your words, but what they truly experience, and sense is your attitude. He emphasizes that charisma isn't only the ability to communicate verbally but also the capacity to elicit feelings in other people. Your demeanor and vitality significantly affect your interactions.

Charisma starts with a genuine interest in others. Dale Carnegie, author of *How to Win Friends and Influence People*, said, "You can make more friends in two months by becoming interested in other people than you can in two years by trying to get other people interested in you." This might be the essence of charisma: shifting focus from yourself to others.

Most people are so wrapped up in their thoughts that they rarely hear what others are saying. Charismatic people make others feel heard. They ask questions, they listen, and they respond thoughtfully. This doesn't just make others like you more—it makes you more likable.

Methods for Cultivating Charisma

Truly Listen to People

Empathy starts with listening—not just waiting for your turn to speak but being fully present in the conversation. It's about asking thoughtful questions that encourage people to share their experiences and emotions, showing them that their words matter. More than just hearing what they say, it's about understanding the feelings behind their words and why they hold meaning. When you take the time to see things from their perspective and acknowledge their emotions, you create a deeper, more genuine connection built on trust and mutual respect.

Want to develop your presence? Then learn how to be completely present when you're with someone. Give them your undivided attention—put the phone down, make eye contact, and just stay in the moment. It's not always easy, especially with so many distractions, but people notice when you're there with them and even quicker when you're not. This presence makes a bigger impact than you know.

As Maya Angelou wisely said, "People will forget what you said, people will forget what you did, but people will never forget how you made them feel."

If you want to be more expressive, focus on how you communicate, not just what you say. Use your tone, gestures, and even your facial expressions to make your words more meaningful. And don't forget about the nonverbal cues—body language speaks much louder than words.

Show Appreciation

Make it a daily habit to recognize and appreciate the good—whether in people, situations, or the little moments that often go unnoticed. A sincere *"thank you"* or a thoughtful compliment can leave a lasting impact. When you focus on the positives and keep an optimistic mindset, your energy shifts and people are naturally drawn to you. It creates an effortless warmth that makes interactions more meaningful and leaves others feeling uplifted in your presence.

Remember, charisma is in the subtle moments when someone leaves a conversation feeling lighter, more understood, or just a little better because of how you made them feel.

Embrace the journey of becoming more charismatic and watch as your personal and professional life flourishes with richer, more meaningful connections.

Chapter 16:
Mastering the Flow State

Be like water making its way through cracks. Do not be assertive, but adjust to the object, and you shall find a way around or through it. If nothing within you stays rigid, outward things will disclose themselves.
— Bruce Lee

Flow, frequently referred to as being in the zone, is a concept initially introduced by the psychologist Mihaly Csikszentmihalyi. After studying many artists, mountaineers, athletes, and music composers fully engaged in what they were doing, he identified flow as the optimal state of consciousness in which we feel and perform at our best.

Flow isn't tied to any single activity or art form. It can happen anytime you're fully engaged, where your energy and focus are completely absorbed in the moment. Whether you're painting, solving a complex problem, running, or even cooking, flow occurs when you're so immersed in what you're doing that everything else fades into the background. In those moments, you're at your best, performing at your highest level and feeling deeply connected to the task in front of you.

When I found myself in a sudden flow state, the first thought that came to me was, *"This is where I'm meant to be."* I was writing—not just putting words on a page but truly expressing real and raw emotions. The overthinking, the doubts, the constant second guessing—it all faded away. I was completely present, and, for the first time, it felt effortless. It was like I was in sync with something much bigger than myself. Nothing felt forced or pushed; it all just flowed naturally.

I felt a deep sense of peace and fulfillment, as if I were aligned with my purpose. At that moment, I knew I was doing exactly what I was supposed to be doing. It was incredibly freeing. I wasn't caught up in the past or worrying about the future—I was just here, in the now. And with that presence came an overwhelming sense of joy and gratitude. I'm grateful for the journey that brought me to this point, the lessons I've learned along the way, and the privilege of living a life of purpose.

Now and then, I have a deep sense of clarity—like I can finally see how every challenge, every hardship, was shaping me for this exact point in my life. For this version of me. It feels like unlocking a strength that has always been within me, just waiting for me to trust myself enough to let it flow freely.

Flow can turn even the most ordinary experiences into something extraordinary. Time seems to slip away, and you tap into a level of creativity and performance that feels effortless yet deeply fulfilling. It's a place where everything aligns, and you're fully present, alive, and in sync with the now.

What is it about the flow that makes it so transformative? What are the real benefits, and how can you consistently find your way into this state? Let's unpack the essence of flow and explore practical strategies to help you access it more often to bring out your best self.

The Essence of Flow

When in a flow state, the areas responsible for processing rewards light up, giving you that incredible sense of satisfaction—not just when you reach your goal but as you're immersed in the process itself. It's not just about getting things done; it's about feeling alive and connected to the task at hand. But experts reckon it isn't the only reason being in a flow state feels so good. They've also determined that the flow state shows a significant drop-in activity in brain regions linked to self-focus.

The less you focus on yourself and the more you immerse yourself in pursuing your goals, the happier you feel. That's the magic of being in a state of flow.

Being in flow doesn't require much energy. Research shows that once you reach this state, everything feels almost effortless. You're at your most productive, but it doesn't feel like a grind—it feels natural, like you're in perfect sync with the task at hand.

According to Csikszentmihalyi, flow is the state in which action and awareness merge, resulting in a seamless experience in which you are both the observer and the creator of your own reality. He further emphasizes that flow isn't only about performance, but also about discovering joy in the process of engaging with life. He describes flow as the key to true fulfillment, emphasizing that our engagement in flow matters more in shaping a meaningful and enjoyable life than the pursuit of happiness alone.

One of the most important elements of flow is complete and total focus. While in a flow state, your attention is entirely locked in on the task at hand. This kind of powerful concentration channels all your mental energy into a single, productive stream, which is why flow feels so effective and rewarding.

Another key ingredient is having a clear goal. You don't have to second-guess yourself when you know what you want to accomplish and how to get there. That clarity keeps you grounded and lets you stay engaged without unnecessary distractions pulling you out of the moment.

Flow also provides instant feedback, whether from the task itself or your own performance. This feedback loop—whether positive or negative—keeps you engaged, motivated, and able to adjust in real time. This balance of focus, clear direction, and continuous feedback makes flow transformative and energizing.

Flow happens when there's a perfect balance between the challenge of what you're doing and your skill level. If something is too easy, boredom sets in. If it's too hard, frustration or anxiety can take over. Flow occurs when the challenge is just right—enough to stretch your abilities but not so much that it outweighs your capabilities.

When you're in the flow, you no longer perceive yourself as a separate entity. This is sometimes referred to as a loss of self-consciousness. It indicates that you're so engrossed in your activity that any feelings of insecurity or self-doubt cease to exist at that moment.

Flow also alters your perception of time. Hours can pass in what feels like minutes, or you might accomplish more than you thought possible in a short span of time. This time distortion is a defining characteristic of flow—where the usual sense of time fades, and you become fully absorbed in the moment.

Perhaps the most rewarding aspect of flow is that the activity becomes the reward. You're not driven by external validation or recognition—the joy, satisfaction, and fulfillment of doing the task keeps you engaged. Flow is about the process, not the result, and it's what makes those moments feel so deeply satisfying.

One of the most valuable benefits of flow is how it naturally brings you to the state of peak performance. Whether you're playing a sport, tackling a creative project, or pushing yourself during a workout, flow allows you to tap into your full potential and achieve effortless and exceptional results.

Activities that induce flow are inherently more enjoyable than those that do not. Because of the profound engagement and sense of accomplishment experienced when one is in flow, these activities are extremely fulfilling and ultimately increase overall happiness.

Flow allows you to escape the stresses of everyday life. When you're present in the moment, worries and outside pressures fade into the background. You're so engaged in the task that you find yourself in a space of calm and balance.

Cultivating a Flow State

The likelihood of entering a flow state increases when four key conditions are met:

1. **Enjoyment:** You genuinely enjoy the activity you're engaging in.

2. **Challenge:** The task should be challenging enough to hold your attention but not so difficult that it becomes overwhelming.

3. **Skill Level:** You need to have some level of skill or competence in the activity.

4. **Process Focus:** Your attention should be on the process, not the end result or the outcome.

When these pieces come together, you're much more likely to find yourself in that state of effortless focus and creativity.

Steve Jobs said, "The only way to do great work is to love what you do. If you haven't found it yet, keep looking. Don't settle." Steve Jobs often highlighted the power of intrinsic motivation in finding flow. The key is to engage in work that genuinely excites you—work that feels meaningful and fuels your passion. When you enjoy what you're doing, it's much easier to get into that state of deep focus where everything just clicks.

To bring flow into your daily work life, start by identifying the aspects of your job that align with your strengths and interests. Setting clear goals and creating an environment that supports deep, uninterrupted focus can help you tap into flow more often. The result? Increased productivity and a greater sense of satisfaction—not just from what you achieve, but from the process of getting there.

Athletes often experience flow during games and physical activities, especially when they're at their peak performance. To unlock the mental and physical benefits of flow, focus on sports or exercises that challenge you just enough to keep you engaged while still aligning with your skill level.

Approach learning with curiosity and a clear sense of direction. Setting specific goals and immersing yourself in new material allows you to reach a state of flow, making growth and development more natural and rewarding. Seeking immediate feedback helps refine your skills and keeps you engaged in the process.

Practical Steps to Help You Enter a Flow State

1. **Determine your objective:** A clear objective gives you direction and keeps your focus sharp, making it easier to get into flow.

2. **Minimize distractions:** Create a distraction-free environment. Find a quiet space, set boundaries with others, and silence your phone or notifications to help you stay fully focused.

3. **Break it down:** Large tasks can feel overwhelming. Breaking them into smaller, manageable steps helps you build momentum and stay engaged without feeling stuck or intimidated.

4. **Identify your peak-performance window:** We all have a certain time of day when we're usually more productive. Some are early birds, and others night owls. Knowing when that time is for you and making the most of it matters.

5. **Find the best time to recover:** Similarly, we all also have a time of day (or night) when we recover faster and can get up more refreshed. Again, for some, that happens when they go early to bed, while others have to sleep in. Some take naps, and others wake up groggy from their naps. When is your most effective recovery time, and how can you make the most of this time slot?

6. **Do what you love:** Engaging in activities you're passionate about is one of the most natural ways to experience flow. When you enjoy what you're doing, it's easy to lose yourself in the moment and find that state of deep focus.

By weaving these steps into your daily routine, you'll create the ideal conditions for accessing flow more often, making your work and life more rewarding.

When it comes to achieving flow and peak performance, Bruce Lee, the legendary martial artist, emphasized the significance of intense focus. Lee said, "The successful warrior is the average man, with laser-like focus."

Flow isn't just a fleeting experience—it's a powerful way to connect with life on a deeper level. By cultivating the right conditions, you can access this state more often and make it a regular part of your routine.

When you embrace flow, even ordinary tasks can become opportunities for growth, creativity, and connection. Over time, this practice can lead to a life that feels more meaningful, rewarding, and aligned with who you are.

Conclusion

As you reach the final pages, take a moment to reflect. You've come this far for a reason. This isn't just the end of a book; it's the beginning of a new chapter in your journey. You showed up for yourself in a big, meaningful way. You decided it was time to stop just getting by and step into something bigger—something that feels true to who you are mentally, spiritually, and emotionally.

You've begun releasing the defenses that once felt necessary but now stand in your way. That takes courage. It's not easy to unlearn old protections and step into something new, but you're doing it. So, pause for a moment and recognize how far you've come—the work, the growth, and the strength it took to get here.

Reclaiming Your Heart

You know what the need to protect your heart feels like. You also know that the need to keep yourself safe can become an obsession, something you hold onto for dear life, as life has taught you that you need armor—something to guard your heart against the world's inevitable pain, disappointments, and betrayals.

Sometimes this armor means being emotionally distant and always keeping people at arm's length. It's a lonely place, but at least you won't get hurt, right? Others find protection in perfectionism or controlling behaviors. It's how you can manage vulnerable situations.

One of the most powerful symbols of this kind of emotional armor is found in the classic story of the Tin Man. He's one of Dorothy's friends in *The Wizard of Oz*. At first, he's frozen in place, immobile because he's rusted solid. His outer shell, made of shiny metal, seems strong, but it's hollow, disconnected, and lacks the one thing he desires most: a heart.

The Tin Man believes that without a heart, he can't love, connect with others, or feel any emotions. It becomes what defines him. His entire identity is shaped around his shell and the emptiness inside.

But as the story unfolds, we notice his kindness, care, and deep compassion for others. Although it's clear that he has a heart, he fails to see this truth for himself. He's too fixated on what he thinks he is than who he truly is.

Like the Tin Man, many believe we need something outside of ourselves to feel whole—to feel worthy of love. We believe that we're missing something fundamental or that there's a part of us that's broken or incomplete because life's disappointments, traumas, and societal expectations shape our perception of ourselves. When we experience rejection, heartbreak, or failure, we start to believe that something must be inherently wrong with us. We compare ourselves to others, absorbing the idea that we need to be more—more lovable, more successful, more whole. So, we put on armor to protect ourselves from being hurt or exposed, but also to hide our true selves from the world, for their rejection is too much to fathom.

Like the Tin Man, the heart you think you're missing is already there. You haven't lost it—you've just buried it under layers of protection.

You've spent years, maybe decades, protecting yourself from feeling vulnerable. By doing so, you've also cut yourself off from the very experiences that make life rich and fulfilling—love, connection, intimacy, and joy.

The Tin Man teaches us that vulnerability is about recognizing what we already have within. He never got a heart; he realized his capacity to love and connect was there all along. He just needed to let himself feel it.

Now, here's the real question: What would happen if you let yourself take off your armor? What if you open your heart and allow others to see you? What if you trust someone with your emotions? It's scary, right?

But isn't it scarier to go through life feeling disconnected, numb, and alone?

Isn't it scarier to wake up one day and realize you've been so busy protecting yourself from the pain that you've also missed out on the joy? What is the point of feeling safe, but being hollow?

At the end of *The Wizard of Oz*, when the Wizard finally offers the Tin Man his heart, it's not a physical organ that changes him—it's the recognition that he already possessed everything he needed to love. The Wizard's "gift" is merely a symbol, a way of showing him that his heart was never missing. His ability to love, to care, to connect—it was there the entire time.

The same goes for you. Are you still waiting for permission to lay down your armor? To embrace vulnerability as your greatest strength?

Remember, vulnerability isn't weakness. It's the key to connection and the path to real joy. It's the only way to live a full, wholehearted life. By softening your defenses, by allowing yourself to be seen as you truly are, you're not losing your strength—you're reclaiming it.

The Tin Man's journey wasn't about becoming something he wasn't—it was about remembering who he already was. It's time to let go of the belief that you're incomplete in some way. It's time to take off the emotional armor that has been weighing you down and trust that your heart—the one you've had all along—is more powerful than you ever realized.

The Tin Man teaches us it's time to embrace our own journey and trust that true strength lies not in armor, but in gentleness.

The path to growth and healing is rarely linear. There will be days when retreating behind your armor feels safer and when vulnerability feels too raw. But let me remind you: true strength isn't found in the walls we build—it's found in the courage to let them down. It's in your ability to stay open, even when life feels overwhelming, and to trust that you're enough, just as you are.

I would be remiss if I didn't take a moment to talk about my brother. We grew up in the same home, yet in many ways, it felt like we were living in two different worlds. We've always had our own perspectives, our own ways of navigating life. As kids, we bickered constantly—as siblings often do. Even now, our playful competitiveness pushes us to strive harder, do better, be better. And honestly? I've come to love that about us. That fire has fueled us both more than we probably realize.

Beneath all those differences is a bond that's never wavered. As we've gotten older we've learned how to be more vulnerable with each other, and that openness has brought real healing, deepened our connection, and created a strong foundation of mutual respect, love and support.

We may not always agree, and perhaps we never will, but there's one truth we both share: family is everything. It's our anchor. It's our foundation. Without it, we wouldn't be the people we are today. He's given me a family I never knew I needed, and watching the man, partner, and father he has become fills me with immense pride and joy. Even when he gets on my nerves (which, let's be honest, still happens often), I love him with my entire heart. I know that what we share is built on genuine love and understanding. He is one of the greatest blessings in my life, and I am forever grateful to walk this journey together.

We all build armor—it's how we survive. Perhaps it came from growing up in a tough environment, dealing with heartbreak, or just trying to get through a world that doesn't always feel kind or safe. That armor kept you going when you needed it. It served its purpose. But surviving? That's not the same as living.

At some point, those walls you've built to protect yourself start holding you back. The armor gets heavy and keeps you from feeling the full spectrum of life—joy, pain, uncertainty, and everything in between. Living means stepping out from behind those walls, letting yourself be open, and trusting that you'll be okay, even if you don't believe it now.

What Comes Next?

This journey isn't meant to be walked alone. I encourage you to share what you've learned with others. Sharing deepens your growth and sends ripples of healing and connection into the world around you. The strength you've found in being soft and open is powerful—it's magnetic. When you choose to heal, you inspire others to do the same. Together, let's create the change that brightens the world.

The process of self-discovery and growth is a lifelong journey. There's always more to learn, more healing to do, and more ways to keep evolving. Here's the good news—you're no longer starting from scratch. You now have the tools, the self-awareness, and the understanding that vulnerability isn't a weakness. It's actually your greatest strength.

So, where do you go from here?

- **Be vulnerable**: In your relationships, work, and even yourself. It's not always easy, but it's where the magic happens.

- **Push yourself:** Push past your boundaries and see what's waiting for you on the other side. Growth starts right where your comfort zone ends. Waiting for you to claim it.

- **Stay open**: To love, connect, and even "failure". Life is messy, but it's also beautiful when you allow yourself to feel all of it.

My Final Call to You

As you move forward, remember that you're worthy of so much more than just getting by. You deserve a life full of joy, purpose, and deep, meaningful connections. It all starts with one choice — *your* choice. The choice is to keep growing, healing, and becoming who you are.

So go for it. Take the leap. That dream that tugs at your heart. It's not random — it's a calling. And you are more than ready. Everything you need is already within you. The strength, the resilience, the wisdom — it's yours. The only thing left is to trust yourself

And if you ever need guidance along the way, I'm here. As a coach, my mission is to support and empower you through this journey. Whether you need clarity, encouragement, or the right tools to keep moving forward, you don't have to do it alone.

With love, always,

Eileen Jimenez

www.ingramcontent.com/pod-product-compliance
Lightning Source LLC
Chambersburg PA
CBHW061733120626
46550CB00005B/1788